Jo Frost's Toddler Rules

JO FROST'S

TODDLER RULES

Your 5-Step Guide
to Shaping Proper Behaviour

Jo Frost

This edition first published in Great Britain in 2014 by
Orion Books
an imprint of the Orion Publishing Group Ltd
Orion House, 5 Upper St Martin's Lane,
London WC2H 9EA
An Hachette UK Company

1 3 5 7 9 10 8 6 4 2

A CIP catalogue record for this book is available
from the British Library.

ISBN: 978 1 4091 5847 9

Printed and bound in Great Britain by CPI Group (UK), Croydon CR0 4YY

The Orion Publishing Group's policy is to use papers that are natural,
renewable and recyclable and made from wood grown in sustainable forests.
The logging and manufacturing processes are expected to conform to the
environmental regulations of the country of origin.

Note: All children are unique and this book is not intended to be a substitute for
the advice of your doctor or health visitor who should be consulted on toddler
matters, especially when a child shows any sign of illness or unusual behaviour.
Neither the publisher nor the author accepts any legal responsibility for any
personal injury or other damage or loss arising from the use or misuse of the
information and advice in this book.

Every effort has been made to fulfil requirements with regard to reproducing
copyright material. The author and publisher will be glad to rectify any
omissions at the earliest opportunity.

www.orionbooks.co.uk

To the special angels who love, protect and guide me from above.
Thank you! I love and miss you very much.

When you reach the end of your rope, tie a knot and hang on.

—UNKNOWN

Contents

Introduction

Welcome! For years parents have watched from their living rooms as I helped parents transform the troublesome behaviour of children and bring more peace and harmony to families. You've seen me give advice to quickly resolve problems with hitting, throwing and spitting; with children who won't stay in bed or who refuse to eat vegetables; with kids who won't listen. And time and time again, when I am out in public, people come up to me and say, 'I don't know how you do that, but it works.'

The truth is that twenty-five years of experience with helping families has allowed me to develop strategies and solutions that work with kids in the heat of the moment. My vantage point in the home – working with children and watching how their parents interact with them – has repeatedly afforded me the perspective to see what's really going on in a family, not just understand child behaviour via textbook standards. More than just a loving nanny, I've been a family troubleshooter!

You love your children and feel emotionally connected to them in every way. You want what's best for them, even if you don't know how to achieve it. That's how it should be. However, because of your closeness – and possibly because of worries or expectations you carry into the relationship from your own upbringing – you can sometimes fail to see what I can see. That doesn't mean, however, that I can't teach you what I know and help you gain your footing, because I can! In writing down what I've learned and organising my thoughts into five easy-to-use rules, I can be in your pocket all the time, whispering to you the secrets of getting it right. Embracing my toddler rules will give you what you need to know to keep your darling little ones headed in the right direction so that they become the kind, well-behaved, respectful individuals you'd like them to be.

You may be surprised to see that four of my five rules are not what you might immediately associate with behaviour. You may wonder why in a book on shaping behaviour we are going to talk about sleep, eating, going out and learning. That's because I have observed that what seems like a behaviour problem can actually be a result of an issue in one or more of these other areas. If parents don't put these fundamentals in place consistently, it's not reasonable to expect your children to be well-behaved. My fifth rule is about good behaviour in and of itself – how setting expectations and modelling them in your own behaviour gives children the gift of an example to follow. In the chapters devoted to each topic, I promise to outline the why and how of my rules, and give you ideas for how to handle the inevitable challenges (to your authority, to your consistency) that will sometimes be a part of their implementation.

Of course, it goes without saying that even with the most consistent and Rule-following parents, toddlers sometimes have a will that defies all logic, and you'll see them act out in surprising and most definitely alarming ways. I can hear you asking me, 'Is that natural?' The answer is yes. Toddlers are supposed to explore and test limits and learn about the world by pushing those limits. Remember, the goal here is not to make your toddler into a person who has to live and breathe within a rigid box that suffocates his or her spirit and personality. Rather, the goal here is for you as parents to understand the toddler rules and implement them as often, as calmly, and as consistently as you can, and to have my tools in your back pocket to use when your toddler shows defiant behaviour.

If you watched *Supernanny*, *Extreme Parental Guidance* or *Family S.O.S. with Jo Frost*, you will have heard me say to parents, 'You need to SOS.' In this book for the first time, I will teach you the details of what that means and break down my SOS technique for being a calm, compassionate and in-charge parent. SOS stands for Step Back, Observe and Step In. I will teach you to be able to do this quickly – we'll make it second nature to you, so whether your toddler won't stay in bed at night, refuses his vegetables or throws a tantrum at the shops, you'll be able to assess what's *really* going on and act accordingly. Trust me, this is what I do with every family when the mud hits the fan – and you can too.

Because thousands of parents ask me how to handle tantrums, I also offer a special section at the end of this book that is devoted to those upsetting and sometimes embarrassing outbursts that are so often the domain of toddlers. After years of observation, I've discovered there are three types of tantrums, and I believe it's vital that you be able to assess which type you're dealing with. Living with a toddler, you'll no doubt experience all three types, but once you know which kind of tantrum you're seeing, you will be well equipped to put an end to it quickly and head it off at the pass in the future!

Raising children is not to be underestimated. Because our children need so much from us all the time, it takes discipline on your part to consistently meet your child's needs on a daily basis. I call that being a disciplined parent. Something you will become better at. And part of what a disciplined parent must do is to be a disciplinarian when a child misbehaves. I believe strongly that it is now an important time for parents to let go of the stigma attached to the words *discipline* and *disciplinarian*. I want you to feel proud to say, 'I'm a parent who disciplines when necessary', because you understand it's part of what your child needs from you. The good news is that when you put the basics in place and learn to SOS, many of the behaviour problems you may have with your children will diminish or even disappear. I'm incredibly passionate about sharing this approach with you not only so that you can provide the best for your child but also so that you can truly enjoy the experience of raising your little cherub and feel proud of being the parent you are. Regardless of how you were raised, this is your time.

Most parents tell me parenting is the hardest job they've ever had to do, but the most rewarding: the job they feel the proudest of. It is my hope that what you read in these pages will help you become not only a more disciplined parent in giving your children what they need but also a more confident parent because you understand why these fundamentals matter and how to provide them – and, as a result, you become fulfilled and harmonious as a family. Where there is hope, there is always a parent willing to learn and make a difference. Enjoy the read!

Jo Frost

PART 1

Disciplined Parenting
Versus
Punishing

ONE

The Five Rules of Disciplined Parenting

I'm sure you remember the overwhelming feeling of love you experienced when your child was first placed in your arms, that animalistic feeling of wanting to protect. I bet you also remember the tremendous sense of responsibility to get it right as well, the realisation that this tiny being is totally dependent on you and you want to give him everything he needs and be the best parent possible. Throughout the first twelve months or so of your baby's life, you were focused on meeting her needs for sleep, food and stimulation, as well as all the other developmental milestones that come in that first year. Once you figured out what her various cries meant and a schedule to meet those needs, life with your little one made you a bit more confident, didn't it? You felt proud you got through the first year and adjusted well, with thousands of photos to prove it.

Then she starts walking and one day, as you're trying to get her to do something – perhaps get her clothes on, or get her into her car seat – it happens. She digs in her heels and throws a wobbly: kicking like a Premier League football player, screaming at the top of her lungs, throwing herself down on the ground. Hello . . . and welcome to the toddler tantrum.

But it isn't just tantrums you have to deal with now. Suddenly you have a Mini-Me who tells you what she does and doesn't want. She's a bundle of contradictions. She wants independence – and she wants you to do everything for her. One minute it's 'Feed me!' – the next she's refusing to eat. She wants to pour her own milk, but it spills all over. She wants to get out of the buggy and walk, but she won't stay by your side and you're afraid she'll dart out into the street. She's learned the power of the word *no* and uses it as frequently as possible: no, she doesn't want to go to bed; no, she doesn't want to share her toy; no, she doesn't want to sit at the table in the restaurant . . . No, no, no, no.

Now what you need to give your child is more challenging than ever before. You want to give her all she needs in order to grow into a happy, healthy, productive adult with good morals, healthy boundaries and the ability to function well in the world. You see the long-term vision in your mind. And you still want to be the best parent possible so that one day when she's grown, she'll look back and say, 'You did a good job, Mum. Thank you.' Parents know that when you have a child you get the title, but here's where you start to earn it.

Take a moment now and think of a picture that represents your desire to give your child the best. Is it you and your little one snuggled warm and cozy in bed while you read a story? Is it pushing her on a swing and her belly-laughing in the wind with delight? Is it the classic Christmas card with you and your spouse surrounded by your smiling children? Whatever it is, take a moment to visualise it. Freeze the image. See it in colour. Experience how happy and content that picture makes you feel.

That picture *is* possible. You can have it. But it takes knowing what fundamentals you need to put in place, the skills you must have to get there, and the discipline to do what's needed day after day for years. Remember, you're aiming to be a conscious parent to your toddler, the person who consistently provides for your child. To achieve this, you have to make sure your child has:

- The right amount of sleep
- Consistent mealtimes with proper portions and the right kinds of foods
- Opportunities for getting out and about, for physical activity, stimulation and socialisation
- Early learning activities to help with child development
- A clear sense of your family's expectations for behaviour, and appropriate corrections when necessary

Of course parenting is 24/7 throughout childhood. But what you give in the toddler years is paramount. That's an incredible responsibility, one that should be held in much regard and respect. You have been given the gift of raising a human being in this life. Not to mention for those of you who already know me, my techniques are tried, tested and proven. You've seen me do them hundreds of times.

So often I hear parents say, 'I don't have the time.' I read somewhere recently that over 40 per cent of today's parents say that they don't have time to think about how to keep their children safe in their own homes. That's so rudimentary that it is inconceivable to me! But if they can't even think of their toddler's physical safety, how can they possibly put these five cornerstones in place? Your interest in this book tells me that you are part of the other 60 per cent – parents who realise the importance of putting in the needed time, and of trying hard to get things right from the start. Not the cliché of 'I've tried, but it doesn't work.'

Imagine you are holding two packs of playing cards. One has cards that say obesity, type 2 diabetes, poor attention and other learning issues, and social relationship problems. The other has cards that say health, learning up to one's potential, fruitful relationships and the ability to function well in the world. Which pack do you want to hand to your child? It's not rocket science, right? I've seen what a lack of these basics does. I've seen children delayed in their speech, arrested in their development, and having trouble socialising with other children. I've seen children frustrated by *wanting* to learn but not being able to because they haven't been taught to sit down and pay attention. I've seen children eat and eat and be given praise for being on their third helping, when it's been shown this overfeeding is a setup for obesity and type 2 diabetes while still in childhood. I've seen two- and three-year-olds who act aggressively and have been given no guidance or boundaries turn into bullies and be kicked out of school at age six.

I know you don't want those consequences for your child, and I also know that what I am asking you to do takes time and energy. That's why I say you need to be a disciplined parent. It takes discipline to feed your child right, to make sure he gets to bed on time, to teach the early learning activities that will stimulate his brain, to teach him how to be out in public safely and to play nicely with others, to reinforce positive behaviour and to curb naughty behaviour. And it takes discipline to create and follow a routine to provide everything you need to in a day. With routine comes organisation, good timekeeping and the ability to do everything that needs to get done, not just for your child but for you too! In doing so, you can all have fun.

I remember a Colorado family I worked with. They were juggling running their household and running their own company out of their house. The mother had no set times for work and focusing on the kids. She felt guilty they weren't getting enough of her attention, so she kept them up too late; as a result, they weren't getting the amount of sleep they needed. Being overtired and missing her led to her youngest getting up in the middle of the night, and she'd feel so guilty that she'd let him stay up, creating more tiredness. I helped her divide her day so that she could do what was necessary with her young ones and still have time to work. That plus putting the Sleep Separation technique (page 72) in place turned the situation around.

THE FIVE-TOOLER

The metaphor I like to use for what parents need to be is a five-tooler. In sport, a five-tooler is a player who excels at five areas of the sport. I'm asking *you* to become a five-tooler – a disciplined parent in the areas of

- eating
- sleeping
- going out
- early learning
- behaviour

A baseball player usually shows strength more in some areas than others, but that doesn't mean he doesn't work on those other areas. You too may find that one or two of the five come easier for you. That's okay. It just indicates where you need to keep improving.

By becoming a five-tooler, you'll become a better parent, one who knows that you are making a profound impact on your little one's life, not just *now* but for later on too. That requires thinking long term. Some parents do this better than others. We live in a society that wants quick turnarounds. But trust me, there are no shortcuts. So many parents are just trying to get through the day or the week. When you think long term, you pull that healthy frozen meal out of the fridge more often rather than running to get a takeaway. You take the time to notice and praise your child for what she's done well. You read that story again even though you're sick of it. And though it may be easier for you when it's eight o'clock at night and you've just come back from some event to tuck her in quickly, you recognise the importance of the bedtime ritual, so you do a shortened version of your usual routine.

WHY ALL FIVE MATTER

These five basic rules are extremely interrelated. If you don't provide healthy food, restful sleep, great socialisation and stimulation, behaviour problems will increase. And if you don't deal effectively with behaviour issues, you will have trouble with bedtimes, eating, getting along with others and sitting still long enough to learn.

Here's an example. When I first started helping families on television, I worked with a young mother who had a little boy. He could not sit down and focus on anything for even *one minute*! When I spoke to him, I wondered, 'Is he partially deaf, or has he just got selective hearing?'

So I tried an experiment. 'Who wants ice cream?' I asked. Well, he heard that! But as soon as I said to him, 'Let's tidy up now,' the words fell on deaf ears. So I knew he *chose* what to listen to. His parents gave him no consequences for naughty behaviour, and because they hadn't got a grip on that, they'd lost the motivation to do early learning activities such as reading to him, because all he wanted to do was damage the book or puzzle.

He didn't have any social skills either, because he'd never been taught to expand his attention, to understand the rules of a game, and to take turns. We were playing Snakes and Ladders, but he couldn't enjoy it because he couldn't sit still long enough to learn how to play. He ended up throwing the board in frustration.

Yes, this child had behaviour issues, but he had learning and socialisation issues as well. I taught his mother how to put boundaries, expectations and consequences in place. I helped her learn how to expand his attention span. I helped her teach him the importance of taking turns with others. I helped her put a good routine in place so that he was getting proper sleep and nutrition at the right times. And last but not least I helped her connect lovingly with him again so that she could praise him, cuddle him and give him love. These efforts, *taken together,* turned the situation around for the better.

LOVE AND AFFECTION TOO!

When talking about the five basic rules, I want to make sure you understand that they are all done with love. I want you not to forget how important it is to hug, to kiss, to cuddle, to speak to your child kindly and with respect. I can tell when children are held and cuddled frequently and given lots of warmth and love – their exterior is soft and their spirit fed. I've spoken to parents who say they were never hugged as children, so being affectionate may not come naturally. And I know that when kids are misbehaving and parents don't know what to do, they can unconsciously withdraw from their children and therefore give fewer cuddles and hugs. When you've had a difficult time with your child, in addition to disciplining when necessary, make sure to surround him with your love. Detach his behaviour from his core. Hug him, kiss him, hold him. He will soften and the bond between you will grow stronger.

I remember working with a family of five kids headed by a single mother whose husband had just walked out on her. She said, 'The kids are being so naughty. I just can't get them to behave.' I saw her kids throwing food at the table, not going to bed at night, hitting and fighting. I mean, everything needed sorting out!

What those kids needed most, before I could do anything else, was love, comfort and stability. They missed their dad and were acting out as a result. I gave lots of cuddles and hugs. When they got angry and threw something, instead of going onto the Naughty Step (a form of time-out that I'll talk about later), they went into a corner where they could paint, draw or read while they calmed down. After they were comforted and loved, I could then put a healthy routine in place with early learning, proper bedtimes, and so on. As they began to heal, only then did I start to implement discipline. Because you hope to heal what's broken, first with love, before the rest can be dealt with.

What Toddlers Need	→	What Parents Need in Order to Give Toddlers What They Need	→	What You Will Gain
Love		Time		Greater willpower
Routine		Commitment		More education
Consistency		Energy		Better understanding
Repetition		Patience		Incentive to continue
Praise		Persistence		Greater sense of support for each other and for your kids
Discipline		Perspective		
Assurance				

CREATING A ROUTINE

As you'll see when I discuss the rule for each basic childhood need, putting routines in place is a common theme. Young children love routine because it's predictable – they know what's coming next. Recently I came across research that backs up my belief. It turns out that when a young child's environment is chaotic or disorderly, it negatively influences the development of her cortex, the part of the brain responsible for good judgment. So the more orderly your daily life, the better support you are providing for her brain to grow well. That's a powerful incentive!

To create a routine, start with a consideration of the amount of sleep your child needs. See page 50 for a list of appropriate total hours of sleep by age. Then work out when she needs to go to sleep and wake up. Schedule the rest around the sleep times: breakfast, getting ready, getting to day care or having morning learning activities, snack, more activities, lunch, nap if she's still doing it, snack, play inside or out, dinner, bedtime ritual, bed. (See the 'Sample Routine' box on page 13 for a sample.) You will clearly see there are two snacks per day, three mealtimes; five and a half hours dedicated to mental and physical activities for your toddler, and one or two nap times or rest periods, depending on age. This also gives you a break as well, time when you can recharge.

Look at the whole week to fold in errands and activities outside the home during the activity periods. Be flexible about the times. If lunch is at 12:15 instead of noon, that's fine. Allow time for your child to transition from one activity to another. A rushed child is a resistant one. Talk your toddler through each phase of the routine. When she knows what will come next, she is less likely to act out and the process through the day is fluid. As she grows, be sure to adjust time and activities based on age and learning needs.

KEEPING FOCUSED

If, after reading this book, you find you need improvement in several of the five essential areas, don't worry – you don't have to

SAMPLE ROUTINE

7:00: Wake up, potty, wash, dress

7:30: Breakfast

8:00–10:00: Morning learning activities

10:00: Snack

10:15–12:00: Morning learning activities, physical play

12:30: Lunch

1:00–3:00: Quiet time or nap (one to one and a half
    hours) if needed, then afternoon activities

3:00: Snack

3:15–4:30: Playtime

4:30–5:00: Supper

5:00–6:00: Quiet activities – puzzles, colouring

6:00: Bath time and beginning of bedtime routine

7:00: In bed, story time

7:30: Bed

put all five in place at once. That's not realistic. If you try to tackle them all at once, you can become overwhelmed.

It's easy for parents to become overwhelmed – not just with raising your family but with your working hours, with having so many chores to do, with the amount of responsibility you've got, or with the number of bills you're dealing with. I understand how stressful life is these days for families. I speak to enough of you every day. Ultimately, though, you can be conscious about making good choices. Sure, some things have to give. But be sure you are savvy about what can give – and what shouldn't.

When I help a family, there's a method to my madness. I might say, 'The food, behaviour, and sleeping are all off track,' and then I draw up a sheet of what the priorities are in order for things to get resolved. Even though sleep is so important, for instance, it might not always be the place to start your focus; if you've got bad behaviour, then your child's probably not going easily to bed and staying there. Of course, sleep deprivation might be part of why your child is acting up. You'll have to be the judge as to which of the five rules needs to be put into place first. As you read this book and understand what needs to change in your family, work out a plan to tackle things one at a time until all five are in place. Ask yourself what small change you can make today that will have a huge impact on your child tomorrow.

If you are reading this book, you want to become more disciplined as a parent so that you can give your toddler what he needs. That's great. But please know that if you've been a pushover – if you've issued empty threats, been inconsistent or had no follow-through, said no and given reasons why but then caved in, given biscuits when she hasn't eaten her dinner, or told her she must stay in her bed but then let her sleep in yours – it will take time and energy on your part to turn things around. It doesn't matter if you are the biological parent, adoptive parent, nanny, grandparent, or other family member. Whatever your reasons for this behaviour in the past – you don't want your child to feel bad, you don't want her to be mad at you, or you feel guilty for not being

FAMILY VISION BOARD

- Think of the picture you brought to mind at the beginning of this chapter.

- Download or cut out images that represent why you want to shape your child's behaviour – your dreams for raising a happy, healthy child, and for having a happy, healthy family. Post them on a bulletin board or piece of cardboard and place the board where you can see it on a daily basis. From time to time, add to it or change it to keep your motivation fresh.

there all day, to name just a few – you can, with consistency, change things for the better.

To get all five rules on track and keep them there requires focus. That's why I suggest you create a Family Vision Board (see box). It will help you remember what really matters to you in raising your family so that the discipline, patience and consistency required to make good choices every day are fuelled by your deepest values, hopes and dreams for your child.

IT'S ALWAYS A JOURNEY

I know that at times the toddler years can be exhausting for parents. Trust me, they were as a professional nanny. Whether you are a stay-at-home parent or tend to your children after a full day at work, you've got to summon up the energy to do what's needed. The one thing that I've learned in my experience with helping families is that even when parents feel like they're at the end of their rope, there's a little bit more rope. It *amazes* me still how much parents can pull from inside themselves to give their child what he needs.

I'm not saying that there are never days when you go and get a take-away or skip the morning's learning activities. If you skip today, though, don't skip tomorrow. There's no such thing as a perfect parent, one who's on point every day. You just want to do the very best that you can and be honest about what you need to work on the next day.

You won't get it right every time. The ultimate parental fear is, 'If I make this choice, will it screw up my kid?' You have to feel your way through. What do I mean when I say that? It's about listening to and trusting your inner voice and not being afraid to make a decision. Sometimes you'll do something like let your child stay up too late, or give in to a tantrum and let him have sweets even though he ate no dinner. Now he's crabby from lack of sleep, or he thinks he can throw a fit and you'll give him what he wants all the time. You realise that was a bad decision and learn for the future.

I'm also not saying that you're never going to get frustrated or impatient. That's normal. When it happens, it's really important to note to yourself how you're feeling and remind yourself of what is important for your kids. This helps you have the resilience to keep on going.

As you read this book, you may realise you haven't provided all of what your child needs up to this point. The good news is we're talking about little ones, a time of life when it is easy to change because their brains have not completely finished developing yet. You can learn to be more disciplined and how to implement discipline more effectively, and you really will affect your child's future for the better.

Perhaps you realise you come from a dysfunctional family and haven't known what to do. You can start fresh today. You can break the mould of your past history and give your child the kind of healthy start that will have a lasting impact not only on her but also on the generations to follow. Imagine the positive legacy you can leave, not just for your family but in the wider society.

It's really true that our children will become the adults who will shape the world to come. They will shape the world in politics, in civil service, in the community. And at the end of the day, really, our mission is to create children who grow into adults capable of making a better world – one with less hate and less crime; one with healthier human beings, greater respect for others, more peace; one where children and adults can thrive.

While I feel strongly about keeping this bigger picture in mind, I also want you to enjoy the journey along the way. Because as hard as it feels sometimes, these years are also tremendously rewarding. Take pleasure every day in providing your child with what she needs, and find joy in all the little moments of silliness and snuggling. Take pride in the moments of success for you as a parent when she's smiling with joy that she's learned something new. These moments are precious and priceless. You know when one is happening because you feel warm and special and realise you will remember it forever.

TWO

Why Discipline . . .
and Why It Matters

D iscipline is a word that has many negative associations. I find that some parents automatically assume that I use the word to refer to the kind of parenting that is uncompromising, strict without any reason, done by people who choose to control their children through physical pain using such methods as smacking, paddling, spanking or hitting.

I want to change that perception here and now because I believe that parents' inner conflict over the idea of discipline has led to lax, inconsistent and ineffective methods of disciplining children, resulting in their being raised without proper limits and boundaries, and ultimately without respect, empathy and compassion for others.

I've come to see that perhaps the issue here is a misunderstanding about the word itself. I use the word *discipline* to describe the corrections parents must make for children when naughty behaviour requires it. In this chapter I will explain what discipline is, why it's so important, and why there's been such a stigma attached to it. By the end, I hope you'll be able to proudly say, 'Yes, I am a disciplinarian!'

DISCIPLINE BASICS

Let's start with what discipline actually is in the context of reacting to a child's actions. People usually equate it with hard punishment, but according to the dictionary, the first meaning is 'orderly training.' And that's exactly what you're doing when you discipline properly. You're training your child to have better behaviour. You are teaching him morals and values that will stay with him for life. You do that not only by setting up rules, boundaries and expectations for proper behaviour (which also takes *discipline* on your part) but by having consequences for inappropriate behaviour that, over time, allow him to think about his behaviour in advance and take responsibility for his actions.

If you fail to provide discipline for your young child, he doesn't understand limits and rules. And this leads to him feeling out of control, which results in him acting out even more. Not only will you see *more* misbehaviour from a child who is not disciplined properly, but you will also see greater selfishness and lack of respect towards others. That's because discipline helps a child learn two important aspects of emotional intelligence: self-control (the ability to compose his feelings rather than explode or act out) and empathy (understanding the effect of his behaviour on others and caring about how they might feel).

Without discipline, in many ways a child never advances past the tantruming 'me, me, me' toddler stage. Studies say – and I can confirm from the hundreds of children I've observed – that ultimately a lack of discipline results in a child who feels anxious and confused, one who over time reacts to people in an increasingly violent manner.

These consequences carry over into adulthood. Researchers tell us that when parents fail to discipline, they raise children who are likely to have poorer mental and physical health, higher rates of unemployment, greater rates of drug and alcohol misuse, and a greater incidence of criminal behaviour. These negative consequences result in a great number of the social ills we see today.

You might have read this and thought, 'That won't be my child.' I hope so too! You have the ability and the influence in your child's toddler years to lay a foundation for behaviour and discipline that will protect your child against negative influences later in life. Take advantage of that opportunity. Your child is looking to *you* for guidance now: 'Mum, is this right or is this

KNOW HOW: WHO'S THE DISCIPLINARIAN AT YOUR HOUSE?

If you are a two-parent family, the answer should be both of you. Both of you are raising your children, so both of you should be teaching correct behaviour.

wrong?' 'Dad, is this thumbs-up or thumbs-down?' Discipline is one of the key ways they learn that.

WHY PARENTS AVOID DISCIPLINE

Some parents shy away from disciplining their child out of fear that they will be judged as a person who abuses his or her child. Discipline absolutely must not be physical. I am very much against spanking or other forms of harsh physical punishment. In fact, I'm credited with being responsible for 67 per cent of parents here in the UK now choosing not to spank, by helping them learn effective non-physical discipline techniques.

Another reason I hear that parents don't discipline is that they themselves have come from abusive families and are consciously or unconsciously afraid of repeating the past. Unfortunately, a lot of adults parenting now come from families whose parents were violent physically and/or verbally. They didn't learn effective methods of disciplining and feel that if they discipline their child, it means they aren't loving and nurturing. Even lowering their tone of voice to give a warning may remind them of how they felt when they were verbally abused. If this is true of you, what I want you to know is that if you follow my discipline techniques, it's not abuse, but part of what a loving parent should do. And remember, you're not just disciplining your child – you're putting in place all the other strategies in this book as well, with loving intent, in order to positively develop and encourage her. In this way, you're breaking the cycle of dysfunctional behaviour and giving your child the right start in life.

Other parents shy away from discipline because they misunderstand their role as parent. In a recent survey, one-quarter of parents said 'fear of upsetting their children' led them not to discipline at all, while three in ten parents say they're 'pushovers' where their kids are concerned. This despite also reporting that their children are out of control and that they fear a lack of boundaries will lead to their kids getting into trouble later!

I believe this attitude results in a total failure to meet your responsibilities as a parent. Your role is not to make your child happy every moment of the day regardless of the personal cost, but to raise her to be a thoughtful, kind, productive citizen of the world. Some people would beg to differ, but it's not a choice to discipline or not. Your child needs discipline, just like she needs food and water.

EFFECTIVE AND INEFFECTIVE FORMS OF DISCIPLINE

The parenting website BabyCenter recently did a survey of fifteen hundred mums between the ages of twenty-five and thirty-nine with children ages one to five on how the mothers had been disciplined when they were younger and how they now discipline their children (see chart on next page). The results not only reveal what kinds of 'discipline' parents now use, but a change in what is considered acceptable. I put the word in quotes because only the first three techniques are actually discipline in that they are consequences that teach a child to begin to reflect on her misbehaviour.

As you read my thoughts on each method, think about what you do now and how you might want to change your approach.

DISCIPLINE METHODS BY THE BABYCENTER MUMS SURVEYED	
TIME-OUTS	
31% of their parents did	90% of current mums do or plan to
LOSS OF PRIVILEGES	
78% of their parents did	90% of current mums do or plan to
GROUNDING	
71% of their parents did	52% of current mums do or plan to
SPANKING	
81% of their parents did	49% of current mums do or plan to
YELLING	
68% of their parents did	31% of current mums do or plan to
FORCING AN APOLOGY	
32% of their parents did	24% of current mums plan to
PUT-DOWNS	
16% of their parents did	1% of current mums do or plan to

✓ **Time-Out**

My Naughty Step technique is a form of time-out. (See page 218.) It's highly effective with children once they have enough language to understand what you are saying (starting at about two years old). I specifically designed it to include all of what is necessary to help a child begin to understand the consequences of his behaviour so that at around five or six years old he can be less impulsive and more able to regulate his own behaviour:

- **Warning**. This tells a child that he's doing something naughty and there will be a consequence unless he stops. This gives him a chance to self-correct.

- **Explanation of why he's going onto the Naughty Step.**
  This helps young children link cause ('You hit') and effect
  ('Now you must sit here').
- **Putting him in a specific spot where you can see him.** This
  not only helps you make sure he stays put but also helps
  prevent the separation anxiety that comes and goes in early
  childhood. It also allows him to think about why he's on
  the step.
- **Has a set time of one minute per year of age.** This drives
  home the point without putting him in isolation for too
  long. Young children have short attention spans.
- **Revisiting what he did once the time is up.** Again, this will
  help him begin to learn why he's been on the Naughty
  Step.
- **Apology.** He learns that he can redeem his behaviour by
  making amends. It also helps him begin to grow empathy,
  the understanding that other people have feelings.
- **Hugs and kisses.** These show that you don't hold a grudge
  and he's still loved.

✓ Loss of Privilege

This technique can be effective if you've taught the correct behaviour and, when you take something away, you make clear that
the consequence for not following your rule is that your child
loses the chance to have or do something he wants. If there is no
correlation between what he's done and what he loses, nothing is
learned.

Here's an example. I once worked with a mother who had several young children. At one point the children were outside their housing complex riding their ladybird push cars. They were venturing out too far. The mum said, 'Stop! Turn around. It's dangerous.' They chose not to listen to her. So what did this mother do? She took away the cars, saying, 'I'm putting the lady-birds into time-out.' Punishing the cars? I pointed out to her that she was missing the point of taking the cars away. What were the cars going to do? Complain that the kids weren't riding them?

Done improperly, loss of privilege is just a passive way of showing you're angry. Did this mother actually teach her children to listen to her? Absolutely not. To make sure you use removing privileges properly, see my technique on page 225.

✓ **Grounding**

Grounding is a form of loss of privilege – the privilege of freedom and independence to go out and participate in activities you like. It's typically used with older children and teens for whom the loss of freedom is a significant consequence. My Sideline technique (see page 221) is a form of grounding for young ones. When he misbehaves in a group, you ground him from participating in an activity for a minute or two. To be effective, you must explain why he has to sit out and remind him again of what he did wrong and what kind of good behaviour you are expecting when he goes back in to play with everyone.

✗ Spanking

I recently saw a sad YouTube video made over a fence by a neigh-bor capturing a dad playing catch with his three-year-old son. When the boy dropped the ball, the father spanked him. What was that terrified three-year-old child learning? Fear – that he had better not drop the ball, that he must have the hand-eye coor-dination of an eighteen-year-old. The father in that video is being unreasonable, berating and ineffective. I have to question whether that dad was raised in an abusive family, because that behaviour is the kind that's typically passed on. Thirty per cent of abused children go on to abuse their own children. Like many abusive parents, this abusive father found excuses to bully his child even though this type of behaviour does not foster encour-agement and motivation to develop skills but rather hinders them.

Child abuse is a silent epidemic throughout the world. Every day in this country five children die from abuse, and that number has been steadily growing over the last fifteen years. That's simply unacceptable. Many parents who come from abusive families are unaware they've been abused, and they unconsciously carry on the abuse. If you or someone you know is being abusive, please seek help. Call Childline: 0800 1111 or NSPCC: 0808 800 5000.

You may not think spanking is wrong, but if you believe you have a right to spank your child hard and find a good excuse every time for why you do it, that's abuse. Spanking has extremely negative lasting effects (see box on page 28). Not only does it create many problems, but it has no documented positive effects.

It may scare your child into stopping the unwanted behaviour –
at least while he's in your presence. But it does not create
learning.

Here's why. When you try to force good behaviour by spanking, you stop the growth of the good-judgment part of a child's
brain, the prefrontal cortex. Because spanking creates fear, your
child responds from the most primitive part of his brain, the
fight-or-flight part. He's just trying to avoid pain, rather than beginning to think through where his action might lead and
understand the impact on another person. These understandings
don't fully form till early adulthood, but you want to be building
the pathways for them as early as possible. Spanking doesn't support a child's overall healthy emotional and mental development.
If you hit your child, you *cannot* shape his behaviour without
breaking his spirit.

Virtually all parents who spank regularly say they were
spanked and it didn't harm them, as if to justify the behaviour.
However, I know different, and so will others reading this. And,
if you are honest with yourself, is that true? Really? You be the
judge of your honesty, because you can't run from it.

If you spank or smack your child – the word you use for the
physical discipline is irrelevant – think about what behaviour you
do it for. Not listening? Running into the street? Not picking up
toys? Hitting? Whatever it is, this book will help you teach your
child not to do those things in a positive, constructive way that
will not only shape her good behaviour but allow a long-lasting
loving relationship between you to grow.

As a society, we're in the midst of a revolution to stop

EFFECTS OF SPANKING

According to the American Humane Organization, as well as my decades of observation, spanking:

• Increases anxiety and fear

• Hinders the development of empathy and compassion for others

• Makes children angry even if they seem passive

• Heightens aggression towards others

• Decreases willingness to comply with adults

• Harms relationship with parent or caregiver

• Decreases self-esteem

• Teaches that violence is an acceptable way to handle conflict

• Potentially causes unintended physical injury, possibly severe

spanking. It's like what happened with smoking. We've gone from nearly everyone smoking to a total ban in indoor public places. The more educated we become, the better the choices we make. Just look at the difference between the BabyCenter mums and their parents! Let's get the number of parents who spank their children to zero.

✗ Yelling

I don't know one adult who hasn't yelled as a reaction to his or her child being in a dangerous situation. She runs near the street, and you yell to get her out of harm's way. That's a perfectly appropriate involuntary reaction. But yelling as a discipline method is *totally* ineffective because it doesn't give the child a consequence that allows her to reflect on what she's done wrong. And because there is no follow-through of a consequence, your child quickly becomes immune to your raised voice. It just goes in one ear and out the other.

Unfortunately, yelling has become the new spanking among parents who have got the message that they shouldn't hit. But shouting is wrong as well. It comes from a place of trying to control your child's behaviour rather than teach him. And like spanking, it often is a result of the parent's frustration or anger, rather than an opportunity for the child to learn. I'm not saying parents can't have emotions, but if you show out-of-control behaviour by yelling, your kids will mimic you.

✗ Forcing an Apology

An apology by itself, when a parent demands it in the heat of anger, is not a discipline technique because it doesn't teach a child the consequences of her actions. Rather, an apology is an important *part* of the discipline process, a process of thinking and learning in a composed manner. At the end, as a way to redeem yourself, you apologise.

✗ Put-downs

Put-downs are, quite frankly, mean, belittling comments about your child: 'You're just stupid.' 'You're bad.' This is verbal abuse, pure and simple. Such comments destroy self-esteem, as well as the loving relationship between you and your child. They have no place anywhere.

There is a vast difference between put-downs and helping your child begin to understand what he's done: 'I'm really unhappy with the way that you behaved at the party. What do you think wasn't right with the way that you behaved?' A mature five-year-old will be able to respond. When he's younger, you have to provide the thinking for him: 'That really made Billy unhappy when you chose to hit him. Look how you hurt him. That wasn't kind, was it?'

We need to teach empathy to our children. If we did, we wouldn't see rising statistics on bullying in nursery and reception, and kids being kicked out of school at the age of seven!

CONSCIOUS PARENTING

A lot of discipline is passed down unthinkingly through generations – what I call auto-parenting. I'm asking you to become conscious about your parenting, to make good choices based not just on how you were disciplined but on the effect you want to have on your children so they can learn. By conscious, I mean that you are mindful, that you think before you act. You use some of what you've learned from your family, and some you leave behind.

As a conscious parent, you ask yourself, 'What's needed right now?' and because you are mindful, you choose the type of discipline that will give your child the very best – training in responsibility, independence and self-control, on one hand, and empathy and compassion, on the other. In this way, you are shaping your child's behaviour in a positive way.

THREE

The SOS Method

You've now read my overview of the five essential rules I want you to be conscious of as you parent your toddler, and you understand why discipline matters. Now, before we go into depth on each rule, I want to teach you one more thing. On a daily basis with your children, you find yourself in dozens of situations you must respond to appropriately: for instance, your two-year-old son wails, and you walk in and see your three-year-old daughter hovering over him. Or your four-year-old is suddenly getting out of bed at 1am. when he's had no trouble sleeping through the night in years. Or your daughter just turned two and is starting to hit other children. Do you simply react – from anger, fear, stress, tiredness? Or do you give the most useful and effective response?

I have a method I use to understand what your child truly needs in any given moment and when discipline is appropriate

– and when it's not. As you'll see in the chapters that follow, it's my 'master method'. I call it SOS: Step Back, Observe, Step In. I do it naturally in my head whenever I am with a child, and I have taught it to hundreds of parents as well. It's very simple. It actually takes longer to read about it than to do. I consider it thinking on your feet with purpose.

SOS is the greatest tool I know for disciplined parents. It forces you to stay calm, look at the big picture and take the most effective action. Much of parenting is like being a paramedic who has walked into a 999 call: you've got to quickly assess the situation and decide what to do. Experience allows you to be able to diagnose the problem and make decisions more quickly, but of course it's less about speed and more about making the *right* decisions on the spot.

That's where SOS comes in. It's a skill that gets better with practice. Through using it again and again, you become better able to put aside your emotions for a moment and look logically at what's going on. It helps you be more *aware* of a situation without being *caught up* in it. It allows you to become even more

SOS

1. *Step Back* from the situation to get perspective.

2. *Observe* what is actually happening: Who is saying and doing what?

3. *Step In* and make a decision to respond most effectively.

conscious as a parent and know you are making good decisions for your child, in the moment and throughout his toddler years.

Let's look at each step in detail:

STEP BACK

When I say Step Back, I mean it literally – take a step back, at least when you are first learning the technique. Later you can just step back mentally. It goes without saying, of course, that if your child is in any kind of immediate danger – say, he runs off in the shopping centre or is bleeding – your automatic response system will kick in, and you will act instinctively and jump in. At times such as those, Step Back does not – and shouldn't – come into play. Rather, it is for all those moments when your child is doing something frustrating, annoying or naughty and you want to give your best response. Know that while you Step Back, the behaviour will continue until you Observe and then Step In with a course of action. That's okay. Your thoughtful response far outweighs a few more seconds of misbehaviour.

The Step Back is to detach yourself from the situation so that you aren't just responding from your emotions or old patterns from the past, or making snap judgments about what is going on. The distance allows you to emotionally put everything in check so that you can look objectively at the situation. It takes discipline to do this. I've been in situations where my heartstrings are being pulled very strongly. But I know that I cannot effectively resolve the issue if I'm acting on emotion. To Step Back, you want to remove yourself and look at what's going on as if it were on a movie screen and you were watching from the balcony. When you do that, you activate the part of your brain that turns on when you meditate. This gives you more calm and composure to deal with the situation. This is what paramedics and firefighters do all the time. They're *in* the emergency but they are not *freaking out* about it. They are calm and controlled.

The ability to Step Back is important because our brains have two parts that respond to what's going on. One is the limbic system, which is the more instinctive part of the brain. Its role is to save us from harm by allowing us to act without thought. There are times – such as when your child runs off in the shopping centre, as I just described – when it's good to react instinctively. It's a reflex action that can keep you or your child from harm. But it's really only useful in physical emergencies. Otherwise you want your calmest, most logical thinking to help you resolve a situation. That means activating your prefrontal cortex, which is where judgment and critical thinking come from. This part of the brain is not fully formed until adulthood, which is why you want to make sure you're using it when dealing with your child – at least one of you needs to be in your 'right mind'!

When I am first teaching a parent to Step Back, I ask that they go to the corner of the room, because I've learned that for most people, it helps to get some physical distance. As you practise, eventually you can be right in the middle of something with your child and switch your brain to be over there, away from the action, as you mentally Step Back. However you create it, getting distance on the situation is crucial.

OBSERVE

Next, I ask parents to express verbally what they're actually see-ing. I ask people to talk because I know that when they talk out loud, they hear themselves better and are more strongly impacted by what they hear: 'I see kids who are overtired and hungry.' Or 'Meagan and Matt are squabbling over that toy.'

Actually observing and saying what you see is a powerful ac-tion, because so many times parents get caught up in their own feelings of inadequacy (particularly if it's a situation that has gone on for a long while) that they can't really see what is happening. I've lost track of the number of times I've asked parents, 'What are you seeing?' and they tell me how they are feeling. It's not about how you feel but what you see. When you truly see what's happening, then you're in a powerful position to do the right thing.

Observation is not only seeing clearly what's going on but an-alysing why it's happening. After you see what's really going on, you run through a mental checklist of what could be influencing the situation so that you can decide on a course of action. For in-stance, you observe, 'He's whining and complaining, and I realise that it's half an hour past nap time and we've been running in and out of shops for the past ninety minutes.' Then you analyse the situation in terms of what's going on from the inside ('He is start-ing day care and is feeling more insecure, perhaps') and outside ('We're late for his nap'). You also look at his past behaviour to see when else he has done this ('Every time he gets too tired').

Good observation is objective – you notice the facts without blame or guilt: 'We've been doing errands for a long time, and he's tired and bored.' Noticing objectively allows you to know what to do next: 'Get home as quickly as possible so that he can take a nap!'

Avoiding Blame and Guilt in Observation

The Observation step is very different from – and much more useful than – the mental traps I see so many parents fall into:

* Blame: 'Why is he so whiny all the time? Is there something wrong with him? What if he whines forever? How will he ever make friends if he sounds like this all the time?'
* Guilt: 'Why did I miss his nap time? What's wrong with me? I'm trying as hard as I can but I keep messing this up. No wonder he's always whining, I can't do anything right.'

These kinds of thoughts keep you from finding a positive solution. If you catch yourself falling into such negative mental loops, challenge yourself to think like a newspaper reporter. What are the facts of the situation? Facing the facts in a non-emotional way is the best way to create lasting change.

When you Observe, you also think about what you want to achieve in this particular situation. When I see parents in some kind of challenging situation that involves their child, I ask them, 'What do you want?' Often they respond, 'I don't want this.' That doesn't help. If you don't know what you want, how can you possibly create it? When you Observe, take a moment to figure out what you *want* – 'I want my child to sit at the table and finish eating', 'I want my kids to play nicely together', and so on. Once you know what you want, then you can go to the next step.

The ability to Observe is not just important in the heat of the moment but also crucial to learning about how your child thinks, feels, reacts and interacts with others. I've learned *so* much from watching children from the sidelines. I observe their facial expressions, their body language, what they say and how they say it, the energy around them, whether they're excited, whether they are upset, how they respond in different environments and how they respond to different people.

This observation allows you to have more understanding of how your child ticks, to better understand her personality and temperament. It helps you understand whether you need to come down very firmly because you have a strong-willed child or whether a simple no will work. It will help you know when to intervene and when to let your child figure out something on his own rather than jumping in to solve it for him.

The more you Observe, the more you will pick up on and the more connected to your kids you become. It's as simple as that.

Ultimately, what you see when you Observe your child allows you to become more *in tune* with him, which allows you to know how to respond to him adequately. Without that, you're just guessing. For instance, parents often say to me, 'I don't know why he's crying.' Well, if you were Observing, you would know why! You could tell if he was tired or stressed or hungry, because you would be paying attention.

Make no mistake about it: your children Observe *you* very closely. Parents often underestimate how much their little ones pick up on every single detail of their facial expressions, tone of voice and body language. How clever and underestimated children are! Kids pay such close attention because their very lives depend on it. You're the person they totally, completely rely on and trust, so understanding you matters greatly to them. I think it's beautiful that they actually know you so well. I want you to do the same thing for them. To Observe, you have to be in the same room. Even when you're having a conversation with someone else, you're also still looking over at your child. You're not so engrossed that you forget to watch what is going on for and with your child. What is she doing and saying? How is she responding in this environment? What help or boundaries might she need? Observation will let you know what you need to work on, when to back off, and what she's already achieving so that you can give her praise to continue doing more! And that's how you enhance her abilities and potential.

STEP IN

The Step In is the part where you consciously implement whatever it is that you have decided is appropriate to resolve, lessen or improve the situation. You put a boundary in place, pour the milk for her, take your two-year-old out of the sandpit where he's just hit someone, get him home for that nap. In the chapters that follow, I will give you Step In actions appropriate for each of the five rules.

Because you've taken time to Step Back and Observe, you have a better idea of the most effective action to take. You come in as your most skillful self, having calculated what you're going to do and ready to execute. You come in with resolve, with the willingness and commitment to execute relentlessly, until the change happens. You are the voice of reason. That resolve, that conviction, is something your child feels, which helps create change in and of itself. You mean business. You're not wishy-washy or confused. You're decisive and taking action now! Whether it is with discipline or plenty of hugs and cuddles.

The Step In is always an action. Even if it's a conscious decision to let a child work something out on his own, it's still an action, because you are consciously choosing to do nothing. If I'm in a room with a pair of five-year-olds who are squabbling, for instance, and after I Step Back and Observe I know both kids are capable of resolving the situation without anyone getting hurt, I may choose to actively ignore the squabble. That's still a proactive choice.

Choosing to actively ignore is different from ignoring the situation, which is putting your head in the sand and pretending nothing is going on. That's irresponsible parenting, which, unfortunately, we see every day in shopping centres, in shops, and on playgrounds. If you've not done the first two steps, then you can't presume that you are making the wisest choice if you 'do nothing'. That decision must come after careful observation. When you actively ignore a situation, you are still paying close attention to it. In the case of the squabbling kids, for instance, you're not just walking away. You're tuning in to make sure they can resolve it. In the case of a tantrum in the supermarket, you say firmly, 'No, you can't have a toy', then 'That's not okay' when he whines or cries; then you ignore the fallout, occasionally expressing your disapproval if it continues: 'That's enough!' When you're actively ignoring a behaviour and other parents give you glares because they are disgusted with your child's behaviour, don't feel like you have to justify yourself. You know you're dealing with the situation appropriately. If someone says something in an attempt to be helpful, reassure that person you're handling it. And if you see other parents in the shop and wonder if they are actively ignoring, listen: you will hear the parent who is actively ignoring address the situation in a similar way to what I've described, with a verbal expression of disapproval first, whereas parents who have their heads in the sand don't address it at all.

To Step In, it's also important to know when not to take over. Otherwise you become a parent who hovers and overcontrols, and your child regresses in his development and becomes resentful that he can't have more independence. This, again, is where close observation helps. It gives you information about what action will be the most useful.

For instance, a child is heading for a full-blown tantrum over trying to put on his shoe. First I Step Back. Then I Observe: 'What do I see? He's frustrated because he can't get the Velcro strap through the loop. He's got one partway through, but his fingers are stuck. And even though he's frustrated, he's not yet given up.' I ask myself, 'What do I want to achieve?' Him to learn to put on his shoe. So I decide to Step In and verbally encourage and coach him. I say, 'You can do it! Look, the first one is almost done. What if you pull instead of push?'

Of course, in this situation, you are looking at how out of control his frustration is, as well as his age, dexterity and fine motor skills, and assessing if he can really do it. But if you conclude that he can, then the best thing you can do in these circumstances is to encourage him to push through. Unfortunately, parents often interrupt the natural learning cycle because they don't want their children to feel temporarily frustrated. They interpret anything that's not a smile and a giggle as unhappiness that they must fix! Parents also sometimes interrupt the natural learning cycle because they are running late – allowing your toddler to strap on his own shoe may take more time than you feel you have in the morning. It's therefore all that much more important to have a routine in place that allows you the time you may need in such circumstances. If you had to rush your child through getting his shoes on today, adjust the morning routine tomorrow, allotting more time to get out the door.

To Step In effectively, you must allow your children to feel emotion without you feeling that you need to control it. It's okay for your child to feel angry. It's okay for him to be frustrated. Frustration helps him push through adversity, to focus and persevere till he gets it. There's a maturity that comes from that. A child is not psychologically unhappy if he's frustrated. He's just experiencing an emotion in the moment, and if you help him push through, it will lead to more endurance, more stick-to-it-iveness, and the satisfaction of doing it himself.

The ability to focus and push through adversity is an emotional muscle that needs to be trained. When parents Step In and do for their children too readily, they think they're keeping their children from harm. But actually what they are creating in their children is impatience and lack of perseverance and follow-through. Too much 'doing for' leads to mollycoddling, unnecessary overprotection and indulgence, which in turn leads to a child being spoilt and not becoming more self-sufficient and truly confident.

Of course, this is a balancing act. On one hand, you want to trust that your child can work it out, especially if you have been diligent in putting in place all the good disciplined parenting rules. But if you've got unrealistic expectations, that's not possible. If you haven't taught her any of the necessary life skills, you can't assume she'll be able to figure it out. Or if you don't understand where your child is developmentally, you might be asking her to do something that's beyond her ability. Most three-year-olds can't reason, for instance, so you can't leave them to work out their own squabble. But if you've taught her how to share and take turns, by the time she's five you can try seeing how she does on her own.

Parents ask me, 'How will I know if I'm stepping in with the right game plan?' My response is 'make your observation and decide on the solution you feel will work. Then try it. If it doesn't work, then try something else next time.' My hope is that by reading this book and the tips and techniques it contains, you'll have a thorough understanding of what to try in most any circumstance.

As I said at the beginning of this chapter, with practice SOS can take place in the blink of an eye, in the heat of the moment. And you get better and better at it the more you do it. It's a

SOS QUESTIONS

Here are the questions I ask myself to help decide what's happening and what action to take:

- *Observe:* What am I seeing? Why is this happening? What are the people involved feeling? What is this child missing? What am I already doing? What do I want to achieve in this situation?

- *Step In:* What do I need to do to resolve this right now? What do I need to put in place so the problem doesn't continue to happen or so the situation gets better? How do I do this fairly?

positive-reinforcement loop. The next section will give you help in applying SOS in a variety of potentially challenging situations with young children, including sleep, eating, socialisation, early learning and proper behaviour.

REFLECTION AFTER SOS

I'd also like to encourage you to reflect on yourself after an SOS experience. SOS is a way to focus on your child and to offer him the best parenting you can. But it also can be a very helpful way for you to learn about yourself as well. Not in the heat of the moment, when your attention needs to be laser sharp on your child, but afterwards, you can think, 'What did I learn about myself through using this method?'

For instance, 'Well, normally when I hear a lot of noise from my kids, I think they're fighting, and I lose my temper and scream, 'Stop!' But I learned through observation that *actually* what was going on was quite harmless. They were just playing and having fun. No one was fighting. I realise that I assume the worst instead of looking objectively at what's happening. I need to pay more attention to what's really going on before I respond.'

Part of being a disciplined parent is reflecting on yourself so that you can improve. It's like rewinding a recording to replay the action. For instance, you may learn that you have trouble staying patient when your child wants to try something for himself, so you don't give him enough time to work it out himself. Or that you consistently push lunchtime back because you want to get all your housework done, but this results in a lot of tantrums that could be avoided if you served lunch by noon.

There's no better situation than parenting to introduce you to yourself. Kids *really* trigger truths about yourself and who you are as a person. I remember many a parent saying to me, 'I didn't really know myself until I had kids.' This realisation is the truth that empowers you. I love how children innocently give parents the awareness of a virtue they need to learn or an ability they need to grow. It's that weird paradox that kids can bring out the best in you and the worst in you at the same time!

When you start to SOS with your kids, don't be surprised if it spills over into the other areas of your life. You'll find yourself using it in all sorts of challenging situations – whether to achieve a goal you've been wanting to get to, to deal with a friendship you hoped would be better, or to evaluate a business move you're not sure of. The discipline you are creating to face your challenges with your kids can be used to tackle any problem in your life.

PART 2

The Rules for Shaping Proper Behaviour . . . and How to Respond When Kids Push Back

FOUR

Sleep Rules

Making sure your children have enough sleep is as important as providing food and water and keeping them physically safe. However, when I ask parents about sleep, I don't get as a response, 'I'm disciplined about my kids going to bed at the proper time because I understand that getting the right amount of sleep is crucial to their mental, physical and emotional well-being and development.' What I hear instead is, 'They need to go to bed because I've had eight or ten hours with them all day. I'm done!' Or 'I want to put my feet up on the couch after a long day at the office.' Or 'I want to have an evening with my husband at the end of the day!'

I want parents to be disciplined about their children getting sleep for the right reasons. Because when you do, the rest will come. Then having time to yourself or with your partner is a well-deserved bonus! That's why in this chapter, I start by talking

HOW MUCH SLEEP IS NEEDED?

According to a National Sleep Foundation study, 90 per cent of parents think their children are getting enough sleep, but most are not. Are yours? The foundation recommends:

1–3 years old: 12 to 14 hours of sleep in a 24-hour period, including naps

3–5 years old: 11 to 13 hours

5–10 years old: 10 to 11 hours

10–17 years old: 8½ to 9¼ hours

Adults: 7 to 9 hours

about what science knows about the importance of sleep and how much is needed. That way, if you've been neglectful about your children's sleep, you'll now be aware of the consequences and begin making better choices for your kids and yourself as a parent. Then I will offer the basics of how to get your children to bed using a routine that sets the tone for rest and creates the conditions for a good night's sleep for all of you. The next chapter offers specific SOS advice and action steps for when your best effort at creating the necessary conditions falls short of getting or keeping them in bed!

WHY SLEEP MATTERS SO MUCH FOR YOUR CHILD

Everyone has a body clock – when they naturally go to sleep and wake up. Ask any adult and he'll tell you what his desired amount of sleep is, the time that he would like to switch off. We *know* when our bodies want to shut down. But we ignore our body clock and stretch our waking time with longer working hours. We're stretching our children's body clocks as well – according to studies, even nursery school children are getting thirty minutes less sleep per night than they used to. Parents may keep kids up later so they can spend time with them when they get home from the office, but they don't recognise the profound effects of that choice on their little ones' bodies and brains. It affects behaviour, brain development and the ability to learn – even physical health and weight!

Behaviour

When I was a nanny, all the nannies I knew would get together on Mondays and talk about how much harder that day was, because over the weekend parents had let the routine slip to spend time with their children, and now we had to deal with the consequences of our little charges being more irritable and revved up, less able to sit and concentrate, not wanting to listen. They were exhausted, with red-rimmed eyes. It was our job to get them back on schedule and into bed on time. Once we did, the rest of the week went more smoothly on every level.

That's because sleep for little ones is not so much the ending of one day as the beginning of the next. If you get it right on Monday night, you set yourself up for Tuesday being a good day, and so on. Without enough sleep, you are going to have bad behaviour and your child's not going to be able to soak up all she could learn. Going out in public becomes a nightmare because she's running wild, won't listen and may be aggressive towards other kids.

IS IT ADHD OR
IS IT SLEEP DEPRIVATION?

Many experts are now saying that some children diagnosed with ADHD may actually be suffering from
long-term sleep deprivation. Whether the ADHD label is
accurate or not, treating sleep problems may be enough
to improve attention and decrease hyperactivity.

Research has now confirmed what I as a nanny have observed
for decades – lack of sleep causes moodiness, tantrums, hyperactivity, lack of impulse control and an increase in oppositional
behaviour in young children. Bottom line: lack of sleep makes
everything harder! Unlike adults, who tend to get groggy and
slower with fatigue, children get more hyped up. They fight
sleepiness, which causes their bodies to secrete more adrenaline,
so they are physically exhausted and mentally wide awake at the
same time. This can be confusing to parents. Rather than getting
them off to bed at the proper time, since they don't see signs of
sleepiness, they keep children up even later, which only adds to
their hyperactivity and crankiness.

Brain Development and Ability to Learn

Lack of sleep also has profound effects on children's ability to
learn and their overall brain development. That's because a lot of
what happens in a growing child's brain takes place during sleep.
Sleep allows for memories to be moved to long-term storage areas

of the brain. Lack of sleep gets in the way of that. It can also impair the brain's ability to make the necessary connections to learn.

Even small differences in sleep schedule can have a big effect on learning. Dr Monique LeBourgeois of Brown University gave a school-readiness test to pre-kindergarteners. Some she tested on Monday after their parents had let them stay up later on the weekend. Others she tested on other weekdays. For every hour of staying up late, children lost seven points on the test. This is as much mental impairment as caused by lead poisoning!

Sleep also prepares the body to extract the necessary glucose from the bloodstream to maximise focus and attention in the brain. Sleep deprivation impairs the body's ability to do this, so a tired child is not able to pay attention as well as she would otherwise. When a child has had the proper amount of sleep, she has maximum concentration, focus and attention. She can sit still long enough to learn, and she can retain and recall what she learns. Given how much our young ones are learning in the first few years, we want to make sure their brains are in their optimal state so that, like little sponges, they can use everything they are experiencing.

Physical Health and Weight

Proper sleep is also linked to our children's good health – now and throughout their lives. During sleep, the body's energy is restored, the growth of bones, muscles and other bodily tissues is promoted, and the immune system does its repair work. Without the right number of hours of sleep, the immune system doesn't function optimally. That's why there are studies showing an increase in colds and flu, for instance, with a lack of sleep.

Not enough sleep is also related to another critical childhood issue: obesity. New research at the UCLA School of Public Health reveals that the toddler years are a crucial period when lack of nighttime sleep can result in obesity later in childhood. The researchers found that kids who were sleep-deprived between birth and age four had an 80 per cent higher risk of obesity five years later. How much less sleep were these kids getting compared to others? Only forty-five minutes! What more evidence do we need that parents must be disciplined about sleep times?

YOU NEED YOUR SLEEP TOO

And what about you? Are you getting enough sleep? It is estimated that parents lose about two hundred hours of sleep a year due to their children's sleep issues. Sleep deprivation is so awful that I actually believe the British used it as a torture method in the Tower of London during the sixteenth century! The mental, physical and emotional effects on adults are the same as those on children, except that we tend to move more slowly and get groggy rather than amped up. You become irritable with your kids; little things become magnified. Your judgment and decision-making ability are impaired, so it's harder to make good choices. You forget things. You're moodier. Lack of sleep is also connected to depression, which can cause you to start to withdraw from your kids – you're there, but you're not engaged.

Effects on Children of Not Enough Sleep	Effects on Children of Getting Proper Sleep
PHYSICAL	**PHYSICAL**
Tired or more speeded up	More capacity to sit still
Increased risk of becoming obese	More likely to be of correct weight
Decreased immune function – may be more prone to colds and flu	Immune system operating well to fight colds, etc.
MENTAL	**MENTAL**
Shortened attention span	Optimal attention span
Less ability to achieve life skills due to poor concentration	Ability to concentrate
Impaired memory	Memory functioning well
Reduced decision-making ability	Better judgment
EMOTIONAL	**EMOTIONAL**
Moodiness and irritability	Better mood, happier
Temper tantrums	Fewer tantrums
Poor impulse control	Less impulsive
More oppositional and aggressive	More willingness to cooperate
Hypersensitive to stimuli such as noise, textures, bright lights	Less sensitivity to stimuli such as noises, textures, bright lights

And here's the worst news: *lack of sleep impairs your ability to recognise what sleep deprivation is doing to you.* We get deceived because our bodies and minds start to learn how to *cope* with less sleep. But we can't do that forever. In a study done on adults, a scientist gave a number of tests to people who had had only six hours of sleep per night for two weeks. They all claimed to be perfectly fine, but the tests showed they were as impaired as a person who's legally drunk.

Overtired parents can get into bad habits with their children that become *really* challenging to break because they require a discipline that you don't have when you're tired! When you get enough sleep, however, you can tackle problems because you've got enough energy. You feel happier and more resilient. You have more patience. You're able to concentrate and follow through on the things you know you should be doing for and with your children. Following my five rules seems easier, even joyful, rather than a burden.

That's why for me the right amount of sleep comes first for young children. Regulating sleep allows your child to reap the benefits of the early learning and socialising experiences you provide and makes teaching good behaviour that much easier. And it helps you have the capacity to provide the four other rules, which in turn allow the whole family to function well and to really enjoy your lives.

SO WHY IS IT SO HARD TO GET THE KIDS TO GO TO BED AND STAY THERE?

As I explained earlier, kids fight sleep even more when they are tired. If you've gone past when their body clock says it's time to sleep, or if you have been not making sure they get enough hours per night, they get wired and the whole bedtime process becomes more difficult. That's why it's important to align their routine with their body clock. Typically a child of this age has a twelve-hour body clock. If he's up at 7a.m., that means by 7p.m. he needs to be going to sleep. By observing your child, you can begin to tell what his natural clock is.

But even if you align the routine to his body clock, if you are not doing what is necessary during the day for him to use up all his energy through learning activities, socialising and romping around, come bedtime he won't be tired because he's not exhausted himself mentally or physically. Or if he hasn't had the proper meals in the correct quantities, he may still be hungry. That's why all of the five rules go hand in hand. You want to make sure you are providing enough food and stimulation and socialising so that when 7 or 8p.m. rolls around, he's used all of his abilities and capacities for the day.

Still another reason for fighting bedtime is when parents become fed up and say, 'I've had enough! You're going to bed right now!' because they want their own time at the end of the day. Without the wind-down of a bedtime ritual, kids aren't primed for sleep so that zone seems harder to reach.

THE IMPORTANCE OF A BEDTIME RITUAL

The bedtime ritual is a soothing, loving, intimate, stable period of time that sets up a child to have a healthy night's sleep. She knows it's a time when she has you all to herself in a way she doesn't during the day when you are busy with other things. The more consistently the bedtime ritual happens, the more she looks forward to it. This makes it easier to implement healthy sleep patterns because she wants to cooperate with you in order to experience the pleasurable ritual again.

The repetitiveness of a bedtime ritual also creates a profound feeling of being safe and protected. Without it, a young child feels vulnerable and going to sleep is more difficult because she feels nervous. She fears she's going to be left on her own and not taken care of. That's why it's so important to create a strong sense of safety and protection to encourage sleep.

To create an effective bedtime routine, you need to do three things:

- Identify when your child needs to be in bed
- Make a conscious transition that focuses on your child
- Create a bedtime ritual that you follow daily

WHEN TO BED?

Look at the chart on page 50 to find out how much sleep your child needs. Look at when he naturally wakes up and work forward from that to determine when it should be lights out. Then give yourself forty-five to sixty minutes before that to do the ritual. Yes, it takes discipline to create and stick to a regular bedtime. But I hope you now understand why it's so very important to your child's behaviour, health and happiness.

YOUR TRANSITION

Working parents often have problems with getting their kids to bed because they are distracted with work when they come in the door. They're still on the phone while their child's in the bath. Or they're emailing or texting while he's talking. The child recognises that the parent is physically present but not engaged. This creates instability around bedtime and a need for more attention, which makes bedtime more challenging.

Toddlers want *you*. They want your time and attention. They want to talk to you, to interact with you. There is no way that you can *have* that focused interaction and fun with them when you've got work distractions. As much as technology is wonderful in so many ways, it is a *serious* problem when it disconnects you from your children. In order to give your child what he needs at the end of the day, you've got to give him your full focus.

The bedtime ritual is the transition for your child from day to night. And I think it's really important for parents to have a transition ritual as well, from CEO to mummy, or head of human resources to daddy – something to mark that you are switching from working person to parent. People in the military are trained to take their uniform off before they talk to their family so that they don't act like 'Sarge' at home. You can do something similar – take off your tie or change your clothes. If you wear a uniform at work, such as scrubs, change before you go home.

I once worked with a man who was part of a SWAT team. He'd come in the door and his wife would say, 'I want you involved with the kids.' Literally, he couldn't do it. He was dealing

every day with horrific situations that required him to compart-
mentalise his feelings and now he was supposed to magically
turn into a playful dad. I helped him learn that to make the transition, he needed ten minutes alone. He would go upstairs,
change, put his equipment away and listen to a piece of music that
he really liked. Then he would come downstairs, ready to be a
loving daddy and husband. His head had to shift focus and his
body had to let down its guard so that his attitude could be
playful.

Whatever helps create the transition is fine. For some people,
I've suggested breathing exercises on the way home, in their car
or on the train. For others, I recommend a quick shower – there's
something to the old saying 'Wash your day off'. Visualise the
water removing everything from the day and putting you in a
better head space.

What would work for you? Single parents who have to go
straight to the babysitter's can listen to a piece of music on the
way. Or take off or put on some piece of clothing or jewellery that
helps you recognise that you're switching to mummy or daddy
mode. If your kids are at home, have a note at the front door with
the letter *T* for *transition* to remind yourself. Or put it on a sticky
note on the dashboard of your car. If you work at home, close the
door behind you to signal you are leaving work behind. Creating
healthy boundaries at home is a must if your office is there, too.

If you have a partner, talk to him or her about supporting each
other on this. Agree to a signal, like two fingers making a *T* to
remind each other to make a conscious transition. No matter
how you do it, being in 100 per cent parent mode will give your

child the time and attention he needs and make the evening go more smoothly.

THE ELEMENTS OF THE BEDTIME RITUAL

I remember back in my twenties my employers would always joke that I must give their children 'fairy dust' because they settled into bed so easily. But it was really because I understood what they needed as a bedtime ritual that would be conducive to sleep. For me, bath time is always the beginning of the ritual. It provides the end of loud fun, getting out that last ounce of energy before you start to create an environment that allows your child to mentally and physically relax.

After the bath, create a peaceful environment and a calm ambiance. How do I do that? First, I switch off all technology so there are no distractions. There should be no TV in the bedroom.

KNOW HOW:
PREPARATION IS KEY

Prep everything beforehand so that the bedtime ritual can go as easily as possible: put out the pyjamas, get the nappy, pour the milk. That way you don't have to say, "Hold on a minute, I've got to run downstairs." Nothing will break the smoothness of the transition and your concentrated focus on your child from bath to bed. The more organic and fluid the ritual, the more it will help your child wind down and be ready for sleep.

Or make sure it's off. Second, I go into the child's bedroom and dim everything down. I pull blinds down. I put dimmers on or just a lamp. I may – for a younger child – put on a lullaby she likes. I start to talk more slowly and softly.

Some younger toddlers may still have a bottle; let them lean on you in their bedroom as they drink to really relax and unwind. They may have a blankie as well or a favourite stuffed animal to cuddle. My niece loves her bunny.

I used to love doing massage as part of the bedtime ritual. I can still picture the twin girls I used to look after who *loved* being massaged. After bath time, they used to run into the bedroom bare-bottomed, lay their towels down on the floor and fall on their bellies waiting for me. I'd put on their nappies and they'd say, 'Rub my back, Jo-Jo.'

Bedtime is a chance for one-on-one concentrated focus time with your child. Create a nice interactive rapport through doing a calm activity such as a puzzle. It should be something familiar that doesn't take too much concentration because it's the end of the day.

Read a book or two. Or tell her a story you make up and elaborate over time. Or both. Toddlers love stories that incorporate their names: 'There was a pirate ship and Princess So-and-So was steering the ship. . . .' For those who say, 'I'm no good at storytelling,' just incorporate what you did during the day and magnify it. So if you were playing with animal finger puppets, go on safari. Or if you were playing ball outside in the garden, go into a magical garden. Or if you were on a beach with a pail and shovel, tell a story about how a ship suddenly appeared in the water.

Leave your kids with happy, peaceful thoughts, so that when you go out of the room, they feel as secure, safe, protected and loved as possible. If you do the ritual well, the beauty is that you put yourself in that calm place also. Then you're ready for some quiet time of your own!

DEALING WITH MORE THAN ONE CHILD

The age of your children dictates the time they should go to bed. Some parents think that if they've got a child who's thirteen months, he should go to bed the same time as their five-year-old. That's not providing what either child needs.

The best way to manage is to look at the sleep needs of each child and make sure that the younger child's bedtime is in place first. Then consider the other child's routine. If they are close in age and will be going to sleep within thirty minutes of each other, you may want to bathe them at the same time. And you may read to both of them at once. Then, while the younger one's being put to bed, the older one can be in his room looking at a book by himself or doing a puzzle quietly until you come back. Or if you've got a four-year-old and a five-year-old, neither of whom is napping and both of whom seem to need the same hours of sleep, you can do the whole ritual together. If there's a big gap between bedtimes – maybe the younger one should go to bed at seven and the other one at eight – then you've got time to do the whole routine with the younger one before starting with the older. Just make sure that you are doing what is best for each child, not what is easiest for you.

WHEN TIME IS TIGHT

What should you do when something has caused you to get started later than usual? Perhaps you've been at a school function or Dad has returned from a business trip and you are late getting started. You think, 'An hour for the routine! That's going to push out bedtime too far.'

Whatever you do, do not eliminate the steps of the ritual. It works because it's routine. Instead, shave down the time you spend on each step. So whereas your bath time is usually thirty minutes, it can be fifteen minutes. Read one book, not two, or make up a shorter-than-usual story. Work it out so you can get it done in thirty minutes without your children feeling rushed.

The *worst* thing you can do is to show a child that you have no patience for the bedtime ritual: you don't want to read the book, you don't really care about interacting at bath time. Then you'll get resistance, acting up, pushback.

Take a deep breath, look at your watch and pace yourself. Still do the same things, such as saying goodbye to the water as it goes down the drain. Or tell the next installment of the recurring story you've been making up – just make it a bit shorter. Don't try to skip some pages in the book thinking he's too tired to notice. He'll always catch you! The less rushed you feel, the more they'll not even notice the time is shorter.

THE ELEVENISH GET UP TO PEE TECHNIQUE

After your child is dry during the day, here's a way to help your child stay dry through the night:

1. Around 10 or 11p.m. (depending upon when he went to bed), get him up and take him to the potty.
2. Wake him up enough so he's conscious and aware of what's happening.
3. Don't carry him; he should be moving by himself.
4. Escort him to the potty and let him pull down his pants and go.
5. Take him back to bed.
6. Eventually, you won't have to get him up – he'll do it himself.

FIVE

Sleep SOS

Parents can get into all sorts of bad sleep habits with their young child that are difficult to break. You put the TV on to pacify him to sleep. Or you let him stay up till he falls asleep on the living-room sofa. Or you lie down with her in her bed till she falls asleep, so she never learns to self-soothe and go to sleep on her own. Or you let him crawl into your bed in the middle of the night. It's like potty training – when you mess up and aren't consistent, then you really create problems for yourself. Little ones thrive on routine, so if you do something one day, they are going to expect it the next! Well, at least somewhat.

That's why being a disciplined parent is so important – you need discipline to put good sleep habits in place and when things get off track, you need discipline to get back on track. That means following the appropriate techniques to the letter every time. I know from working with hundreds of families that if you do follow my steps precisely, you will meet with success eventually, as I hear from you proud parents all the time on my Twitter.

You already know about the importance of a bedtime routine and how to put one in place. In this chapter, I offer the most common scenarios parents tend to find themselves in at night with their children and how to use my SOS technique to address each one. I think I've covered all the nighttime dramas, but even if you don't see your particular sleep issue addressed, you'll learn how to think about what to do. With every sleep situation, the key is to identify why there's a breakdown in sleep and then create a plan of action using the relevant technique in this chapter. As you can see from the examples, some scenarios are straightforward and require one specific action. Others need a combination of changes.

CRYING IN THE MIDDLE OF THE NIGHT FROM THE COT

Your child is thirteen months old and has been sleeping through the night for months. Suddenly, over the past couple of weeks, she's started waking in the night. You go in, pick her up to comfort her, then put her back into her cot, where she proceeds to scream even more. You pick her up again and rock her till she falls asleep, then carefully put her down once more, hoping not to wake her. Sometimes she wakes up and the process begins all over again. This can go on for hours. You are exhausted but don't know what else to do.

Step Back: Take a breath and don't react.

Observe: Why is she suddenly waking in the night? Is she on a routine where she's consistently having the appropriate amount of milk and food? Is she being stimulated and active enough in the day? Is she teething and in discomfort?

What do you want to achieve? Having your child learn how to put herself back to sleep.

Step In: If you don't have the right mealtimes or food and milk quantities in place, start there first thing tomorrow and make sure you do plenty of activities and offer lots of stimulation during the day.

What can you do *right now*? You may have noticed during the day that her cheeks have been very red. Her nappies have been more stinky than normal. And she may have a bit of nappy rash. She's been dribbling a lot and a bit off her food. That tells me she's teething. If so, you may give your child some teething granules or homeopathic medicine that will calm the inflammation. But the reality is that teething can go on for months. So you need to pick her up to soothe and comfort.

Perhaps you see no sign of teething or your child is old enough for that not to be an issue. Then it would seem that she's just got into the habit of waking and needs to learn to put herself back to sleep. That's when you should put the Controlled Timed Crying technique in place. It's a technique for teaching a child to go to sleep on her own at bedtime, at nap times and when she wakes in the night. It will take no more than a week to work and you must consistently follow the steps. If you're using it in the middle of the night, start with Step 2. The technique can be used from the time they are on solids (eight months) to roughly two years, depending on if they are in a cot or not.

THE CONTROLLED TIMED CRYING TECHNIQUE

1. Kiss your toddler goodnight and then place her in the cot, say goodnight and calmly walk out of the bedroom.

2. The first time you hear her cry, go in, place your hand on her tummy and softly say 'shhh', without making eye contact, then leave the room. Wait five minutes. If she's still crying, repeat the same routine.

3. If she still cries, go back in ten minutes and then, if necessary, twenty minutes after that. It is important you double the time you stay away each time you leave the bedroom.

4. Continue to do the technique, doubling the time as necessary. It should look like this: five minutes, ten minutes, twenty minutes, forty minutes, eighty minutes.

5. Resist picking her up or she'll think she's getting out of bed and when you put her back in the cot she will scream even more.

6. Remember to refrain from talking to her. It won't comfort her and it will only send her a mixed message that you want a conversation. The only noise you should be making is the comforting noise of 'shhh'. This allows her to recognise that it is sleep time, a time when we rest and sleep and do not talk.

AFRAID OF SLEEPING IN OWN BED

You've just moved into a new home. You set up your four-year-old's room first – his bed, his familiar quilt, his stuffed animals. But when you put him to bed, he cries and cries. He's a well-adjusted little boy and doesn't show any anxiety during the day. You've got all the routines in place – sleeping and eating, stimulation, going out for socialisation. Sleeping alone has never been an issue before. You know it's not a good idea to go and sleep in his bed with him. But it's late and you and he are both tired, so what else can you do?

Step Back: Take a deep breath and don't react.

Observe: What's going on? Nothing has changed but his house and his room.

What do you want to achieve? Getting him to sleep comfortably in his own bed.

Step In: In this scenario, this little boy is not yet familiar with his bedroom. That's unsettling for him. During the day, he's fine because you are with him. At night, separation anxiety kicks in because he's alone in a strange place.

The plan of action in this circumstance should be twofold. At night, I suggest you use the Sleep Separation technique (see box on page 72). In this technique, you are there with him until he falls asleep but not interacting with him, gradually removing yourself as he gets used to being in his room.

I remember working with a family with a three-year-old

where both parents worked. The father would get home before the mother but would keep his child up too late because he felt it was a woman's place to be taking care of everything in the home, including putting the kids to bed. His wife was a student as well as working full-time and he had much more time available. I made the father do the Sleep Separation technique on a little mushroom stool in his child's room because he didn't want to sit on the floor. It worked beautifully. Later, he did the Stay in Bed technique (see page 74) because his little boy would wake up an hour after falling asleep and go into the living room, where the dad was watching TV. Having the dad take charge brought the couple closer together and the father and son became closer too.

A lot of parents ask me if it will somehow damage their child emotionally not to verbally respond when he tries to talk to you in a situation like this. The answer is simple and clear: of course not. He's learning that night is a time to be quiet and go to sleep and he's learning how to go to sleep by himself.

Back up the nighttime technique by having him spend time playing in his room with you and by himself during the day so that he gets more familiar with his surroundings. Soon he'll be comfortable and sleeping easily again by himself.

The Sleep Separation technique should also be used when:

- Your child is waking in the night crying and you realise he's become more clingy and needy than usual during the day too. He is going through a stage of separation anxiety.
- You've got into the habit of lying in his bed with him until he falls asleep.

- He's been sleeping with you in your bed and now you are transitioning him to his own room.
- You've just moved him from a cot to a toddler bed and he's unfamiliar with it.

If you are using it when a child wakes in the night, start with Step 2. Whatever the circumstance, make sure you don't end up falling asleep on the floor all night. In order for this technique to work, you need to be moving closer to the door and then out. Sitting in a chair rather than on the floor helps. Again, consistency is key. If you talk to him, if you give in and lie next to him, if you let him into your bed, it's going to take longer.

THE SLEEP SEPARATION TECHNIQUE

1. Complete your usual nighttime routine. After your cuddles and kisses, say goodnight and tell him it's time to close his eyes and go off to sleep.
2. Turn the lights off, leave the door ajar and sit adjacent to his bed or cot, out of arm's reach, in a position where you can be comfortable. Do not get into bed with him.
3. Stay, sitting in silence, until he goes to sleep. If he tries to talk, don't answer him and if he gets out of bed, place him gently back into bed. If he tries to run out of the room, close the bedroom door, so make sure you have a low night-light in the room.
4. Repeat the same steps the next night, but this time sit a little farther away from him, until eventually you are

sitting outside the door with the door open. Then you don't have to do it at all.

You might need to modify this technique depending on your circumstances. I helped a mother once who had adopted two children who had been very traumatised before coming to her. She was very sensitive to their situation, so they slept with her for a long time. Now she wondered how to transition them to their own beds. I had her do the Sleep Separation technique and put her in between the two beds. Then, once they were able to go to sleep on their own, I wanted them to be able to know that they could always come into Mummy's bedroom to make sure she was still there. So I drew big Yeti feet on paper with yellow neon marker that went from their beds into her bedroom and left both doors open. That way, if they were feeling a bit worried or scared, they could follow the feet and find Mum. She would then put them back to bed again. At that point, she used the Stay in Bed technique (see page 74). Her kids needed her quiet but verbal reassurance. So when they followed the yeti feet to her room, she comforted and reassured them, then tucked them back in their own beds. After doing this a few times, they learned they were safe and she would always be there.

WON'T STAY IN BED

Your youngster has never had any sleep issues. He goes to bed at a regular time, falls asleep easily and sleeps through the night. He's just turned three, so you decided to transition him to a toddler bed. But he won't stay there. You tuck him in, but he pops back out of the room like a jack-in-the-box. You put him back, telling him to stay there and a few minutes later he's back again. You have no idea what to do.

Step Back: Take a breath and don't react.

Observe: Is he experiencing separation anxiety? Is anything different in the situation besides the change of bed? Have you taught him to stay in bed?

What do you want to achieve? Him staying in bed.

Step In: This doesn't seem like a child who is experiencing separation anxiety. You are not seeing the signs during the day. The only thing that changed is that you moved him into a bed that allowed him the freedom to run around. But you haven't taught him to stay in bed.

This is a circumstance that calls for the Stay in Bed technique (see below). Use it anytime a child is not experiencing separation anxiety but is finding a thousand excuses to come out of the room. It includes a reward chart (see page 210) as part of the technique. Make sure you don't give the reward till he fills the chart – otherwise he'll think he gets a reward for one good night.

THE STAY IN BED TECHNIQUE

1. When your child gets out of bed, take him back to bed with a simple, 'It's bedtime, darling'. Ignore all excuses except potty – and that only once.

2. The next time he gets up, usher him back with just 'Bedtime'.

3. The third time he gets up, put him back without saying a word. Stay calm. Avoid eye contact, as your eyes speak volumes and don't communicate in any way at any cost. He'll say, 'Why aren't you talking to me?' Say nothing.

4. Repeat again and again if need be; sooner or later he'll give up.

5. Use a reward chart to tick off trouble-free nights. When he gets to four nights without a problem, he can have a reward if you choose. But be sure it is something small and inexpensive; you don't want him acting up to get a prize.

FINDING HER IN YOUR BED

Your four-year-old goes to bed easily. But at some point in the middle of the night, she gets up to pee and then comes into your room and crawls into bed with you. Often you don't even hear her come in but only discover her there in the morning. You know it's a bad habit but are unsure how to deal with it.

Step Back: Take a breath and don't react.

Observe: Is she in the midst of some transition – to preschool, to a different day care setting, after a death in the family, etc. – that might mean she's more needy than usual? Is she sick? Experiencing separation anxiety? What do you do if you do wake

up when she comes in? Let her get into the bed or bring her back
to her own?

*What do you want to achieve? Getting her to go back to sleep in
her own bed if she gets up in the night.*

Step In: Your plan should be to put her back in her own bed
unless she is sick or going through some emotional difficulty.
Those are the only times I recommend that a child sleep with
her parents. How you put her back depends on your observation.
Usually a simple hug and 'Goodnight' suffices. In the morning,
talk to her about how big girls go back to their own beds after
peeing in the night.

If you think this behaviour is being caused by some anxiety
over a transition, use the Sleep Separation technique (page 72) to
offer her reassurance during the change. If it becomes a regular
routine, use the Stay in Bed technique to break the habit. And if
the problem is that she's so quiet that you don't notice when she
crawls into your bed but only realise it when you wake up in the
morning, use my Chimes technique. (See below.)

THE CHIMES TECHNIQUE

1. Put wind chimes or a bell on a string on your bedroom
   door. That way you'll hear him come in.
2. Don't be tempted to bring him into your bed unless he's
   sick or going through some emotional difficulty. Get up
   and take him back to his bed and use the Stay in Bed
   technique if he won't stay there.

SIBLINGS WAKING EACH OTHER UP

Your little one is fourteen months old and has been sleeping in your room. You've now put him with his three-and-a-half-year-old sister. But it hasn't been working out very well. She keeps him up talking to him, then he wakes in the middle of the night crying, which wakes her. Then she wakes up earlier than he does and wakes him up. No one's getting enough sleep, including you!

Step Back: Take a breath and don't react.

Observe: Are you putting them to bed at the same time? Does she know she needs to be quiet and not talk to her brother? Have you taught her what that means and she's not listening? Or does she not understand what she's supposed to do? And why is he waking in the night crying? Is he hungry, meaning he needs more food or milk during the day to sleep through the night? Is he teething?

What do you want to achieve? The two of them sleeping peacefully throughout the night in the same room.

Step In: One- to three-year-olds need twelve to fourteen hours of sleep, while three- to five-year-olds need eleven to thirteen hours. The fact that she's keeping him up and waking before him are signs that they should be having separate bedtimes. You really need two plans – one for him and one for her.

For Him

1. Put him to sleep thirty to sixty minutes before your older one's bedtime so that he will be sound asleep before his sister comes in.

2. Offer a bottle or cup of milk just before bed, but don't forget to brush his teeth.

3. Use the Controlled Timed Crying technique (see page 69) if he wakes in the night. Hopefully it will be no longer than a week before he stops crying at night.

For Her

1. Talk to her about how she needs to be quiet at night and in the early morning in her room. Practise during the younger one's nap time.

2. Make sure you have an established bedtime routine to settle her into the day-to-night transition. Read her a story on your bed or in the living room so that when she goes into the bedroom, she understands it's lights out and no talking because her brother is asleep.

3. Buy her an alarm clock with a fun animal sound and set it for the time your younger one wakes up. Teach her that if she wakes up before the sound, she can come to your room to look at books or do a puzzle quietly but she can't wake up her brother.

4. If she is disobedient and wakes him after you've taught her what to do, use a Loss of Privilege technique, such as no bike riding in the park today. (See page 225.)

ACTING UP IN THE BEDROOM

You have three-year-old twins. You put them to bed at the same time, but instead of going to sleep, they play in their room for hours. You go in and tell them to lie down and be quiet but they're up again in a few seconds. Eventually you lose your temper. All of you are tired and you are at the end of your rope.

Step Back: Take a breath and don't react.

Observe: Are they getting the stimulation they need during the day so that by bedtime they are ready to sleep? What are you doing for stimulation? How much physical activity are they getting? What kinds of activities? Why, when you go in the room and tell them to settle down, do they not do as they are told? Are there consequences to not listening to you? Or do you issue empty threats and never follow through? Do they misbehave just at bedtime or during the day as well? Do they choose not to listen to you just at night or during the day too?

What do you want to achieve? To have them do what they're told when you tell them to go to sleep.

Step In: This situation seems like *Mutiny on the Bounty* to me. There are a number of issues that need to be addressed.

First and most important, it's clear that you don't have the respect of your children. You need to establish your authority. This will not only help with the immediate problem but help your family life overall. You need to establish house rules and consequences for misbehaviour. At the same time, you need to establish healthy sleeping patterns. It also doesn't seem like your children are getting enough stimulation if they are playing in their room for hours. Make sure you're adhering to the Early Learning (page 159) and Social (page 122) rules.

KNOW HOW:
NO NAUGHTY STEP AT NIGHT

All of you who have seen me put youngsters on the Naughty Step (page 218) might be wondering why I don't suggest using the Naughty Step to curb inappropriate behaviour at bedtime. That's because, with sleeping issues, getting a child out of bed and onto the Step gives her a means of staying up. The point is to get her to go to sleep. She gets her own way if you put her on the Step. A loss of privilege has a far greater impact. The next day, when she's up and ready for fun, you say, 'Sorry! We're not going to the pond to feed the ducks, remember? I told you that if you didn't be quiet, you wouldn't go to see the ducks, and you chose not to listen to Daddy, so we're not going now.'

'GOOD' AND 'BAD' NIGHTS

Sometimes it's really hard to get your almost-five-year-old to bed. You keep a consistent routine day after day with respect to mealtimes and bedtime, but some nights are so much harder than others. He resists going to bed and is extremely hyper. Plus he acts out more on certain days than others. It seems to be related to the days he's at nursery, but you are not sure.

Step Back: Take a breath and don't react.

Observe: Exactly when does this behaviour occur? Is it mostly on the days he's at nursery? Is he sleeping at school, so he's less tired on the days he's been to school? How much sleep is he getting at school? How active has he been? Has he used up all of his energy at school and comes in the door worn out? Is there a relationship between how much physical activity he's had that day and how easy or hard it is to get him to bed? Does he come in the door hungry on the days he's at school? When is he the most hyper? What has he done that day?

What do you want to achieve? The proper amount of sleep so that your child will be rested for the next day.

Step In: Routines are important, but you need to adjust them to accommodate the sleep and activities your child has had during the day. If you take your son to nursery three times a week, on those particular days he may come home really hungry and tired, so you push everything slightly earlier by half an hour. But perhaps he's slept for two and a half hours at school, so he's not tired. Then you've got to push bedtime slightly later. Or maybe he's gone to a swimming class afterwards and used up all his energy, so bedtime should be at the normal time.

Keep a close eye on what exactly he is doing every day and adjust your schedule accordingly. When bedtime goes smoothly, you know you got it right that day. Pay attention to what you did in relation to his schedule and do that the next time he's in that circumstance. And remember that in children, hyperactivity can be a sign of being *overtired,* rather than signalling a need for less sleep.

NIGHTTIME FEARS

You have a happy-go-lucky four-year-old who has never had any issues with bedtime. Suddenly she clings to you when you put her to bed and tells you she's afraid of monsters coming in at night. You put a night-light in her room and reassure her that there are no such things as monsters, but as the days pass, she seems to be getting more afraid, not less. Bedtime has become a tug-of-war, with her trying to keep you there as long as possible and you trying to reassure her and leave.

Step Back: Take a breath and don't react.

Observe: Has she been exposed to any TV shows or movies that might have provoked this fear? Or did it arise out of the blue? What kind of bedtime routine do you have? Is it providing enough cuddling time so that when it comes time for bed, she's ready to say goodnight and go to sleep? How do you reassure her when she's afraid? Is she really afraid or saying 'I don't want to sleep now'?

What do you want to achieve? To have your daughter go to sleep without fear.

Step In: This scenario is very common. Between three and four, when children's imaginations are active in full force, it is common for them to suddenly become afraid of monsters, ghosts and/or the dark. This is particularly so if they've seen some scary show that was meant for older children. But even without outside images, such fears can arise.

Fears such as these tend to come out at night because your child is busy during the day. She's got activities that have distracted her. She's playing with friends. When she goes to bed, everything's quiet but her mind's still ticking. That's one of the reasons why I believe in having a good bedtime routine – you want to do your utmost to allow her brain to switch off.

If through Observing you realise that you may need to monitor your child's media intake better, please do that. And if you understand now that you've been shortchanging your child on the bedtime routine and she really needs a bit more of your time and attention, please do that.

But in this scenario, your most important job is to create a sense of safety. You've taken a rational approach, but four-year-olds aren't rational. For her, the monsters are real and no amount of you telling her they're not will change her feelings.

To deal effectively with this situation, you have to enter her world. When you're stroking your child's forehead and being cosy and she starts talking about monsters or bad people breaking in, you've got to be like Superhero Parent: 'Oh, *no* one's going to come in this house! No one would *dare* because Mummy's strong and Mummy wouldn't allow anyone in this house!'

If she's still afraid, rather than denying her feelings, get rid of the monsters so she can sleep safely. Ask her where they are and reassure her that you can get rid of them with your mummy magic. Use your hands and conjure up a saying to banish the monsters where she tells you they are. This creates a sense of protection. I don't think that that's misleading a child; rather, you're giving her what she needs at this point in her development. She needs to feel safe and if that means a little acting, then so be it. Try this: 'Monster, monster, where are you? We're going to sleep, so must you. I'll clap my hands and nod my head so you can go quickly, quickly, to bed.'

THE DUMMY FAIRY TECHNIQUE

Dummies are for infants to help them sleep, not for keeping toddlers quiet. Here's how to put a stop to it:

1. Tell your toddler that 'The Dummy Fairy's coming to-morrow to take the dummy!' and explain why. Parents come up with different stories, such as: 'You're a big girl now . . . ', 'They need them for the babies . . .' and so on. Make it short and sweet (in other words, *not* that her teeth will stick out and it will cost thousands of dollars in orthodontic fees to set them right later on). Toddlers don't understand this kind of reasoning.

2. Collect the dummies with your child and place them in a gift bag.

3. Hang the bag on a doorknob or place in a sitting area.

4. Leave a note for the fairy to take the dummies.

5. When she's asleep, collect bag and put them *all* in the bin outside the house (no chance of you saving one).

6. Leave a small gift inside the bag.

7. If possible, sprinkle a few coloured feathers and some glitter around the bag as evidence that the Dummy Fairy has truly visited.

SIX

Food Rules

What you feed your children matters a lot. As a nanny, I always made sure my little charges ate properly. Eating healthfully is one of my rules because when you give children the right kinds of food, in the right amounts and at the right times, you set them up for everything else in their day to go well – their ability to learn, to have fun with others, to behave well (we've all seen how a hungry toddler can misbehave), even to sleep.

When you feed your child properly, you're giving her body and mind not only what they need for today but also the raw materials for her healthy growth and development throughout her childhood. You're also helping create lifelong eating habits and patterns.

In my experience with parents, however, there's often a sense of detachment between what you feed your child today and what you're setting her up for in adulthood. There are so many years in between that it's hard to see the potential long-term consequences of your choices. That's why it's easy to reach for the frozen pizza again and again. Or to give in on the chips or the sugary dessert to avoid a tantrum in the store. You're busy and you're tired, so you choose the easiest thing.

Of course an occasional cookie, a handful of chips, or one hot dog won't do any real harm. It's when it becomes routine that real damage can be done. And it's not just the possibility of adult obesity, type 2 diabetes, high cholesterol and high blood pressure, with all the associated diseases, but the very real possibility of these conditions in childhood!

We've all heard the horrifying statistics – *childhood obesity has tripled over the last thirty years, with nearly 20 per cent of children ages six to eleven now classified as obese and one in every three children considered overweight or obese.* One in three!

Being overweight or obese in childhood is dangerous. In a sample of obese children five to seventeen years old, 70 per cent had at least one risk factor for cardiovascular disease. Five-year-olds in danger of heart disease! Obese children are also at immediate risk for type 2 diabetes, bone and joint problems, sleep apnea, asthma, liver damage, low self-esteem and poor body image, bullying and teasing. As for long-term consequences, children who are obese are highly likely to be obese as adults and have a greater risk of stroke, heart disease, type 2 diabetes, arthritis and many kinds of cancer. And if a child is overweight before the age of eight, obesity in adulthood is usually more severe.

KNOW YOUR CHILD'S BMI PERCENTILE

Parents are not always aware of whether their child is overweight. That's why it's a good idea when you take her in for her annual physical to find out her BMI (body mass index) percentile. Doctors measure a child's BMI starting at age two and compare it to the weight and height of children of the same age and gender to get a percentile. Healthy weight is considered to be a BMI at the 84th percentile or lower, overweight is a BMI between the 85th and 95th percentiles, and obesity is a BMI at the 95th percentile or greater.

Feeding your children right is your responsibility, because at this point you are in control. When they're adults, they'll make their own decisions, based – you hope – on the great choices you've made when they were young. Right now, you buy the food. You cook for them. You're in charge of the amount they eat. You're the role model; you set the standard of what's appropriate to eat. You child is *watching* you. He sees the choices you make.

I've heard every excuse in the book from parents for not eating healthily: no time, can't cook, kids won't eat it, too expensive, too confusing. I hope this chapter will give you the reasons and the tools to become disciplined about this very important part of your child's life. I am going to show you how you can cook healthy, quick, low-cost meals that your children will eat.

Even if your child is at a normal weight, I urge you to follow a healthy food plan. High-fat, high-sugar diets have health consequences other than obesity. I once worked with a single dad whose children were slim, so he didn't think there was anything wrong with the junk-food diet he served. But it turned out that those young children's cholesterol levels were extremely high. Just because children are not overweight does not mean they're healthy. Once this dad learned about the health risks his choices had created for his kids, he was eager to learn the information I'm going to share with you here.

I know that you are bombarded every day with *so* much information about what's good to eat and what's not that it's easy to feel confused and overwhelmed.

THE FIVE FOOD GROUPS

Because I want to make this easy for you, I have created a 'Rainbow Chart' on page 92. It shows you the five categories of foods that you should be providing on a daily basis to your child: proteins, carbohydrates, fruits and vegetables, dairy and oils. It also gives you a wide variety of foods within each group. Furthermore, it explains how that food group helps your child's physical and mental development. I've paired each group with a colour so it's easy to remember.

HEALTHY STYLES OF COOKING

It's not just what you eat and how much, but the style you cook it in that matters. Steaming, boiling, baking, and grilling are healthier than frying. And oils – olive, canola, corn – are better than butter or lard.

Effects on Children of Eating Poorly	Effects on Children of Eating Healthily
PHYSICAL	**PHYSICAL**
Increased risk of high cholesterol, high blood pressure	More likely to be ideal weight
Increased risk of overweight/obesity	Fewer, if any, serious health problems
Increased risk of type 2 diabetes, heart disease, joint problems, sleep apnea, asthma	Optimal physical stamina
Increased risk as an adult of the above problems plus a wide variety of cancers	Growth is optimised
May grow more slowly	**MENTAL**
Duller skin and hair, less healthy nails	Brain has nutrients for optimal learning
MENTAL	Energy to explore and learn
Brain may not have nutrients for optimal learning	**EMOTIONAL**
May have less energy to learn and explore	Better mood and impulse control because they are eating at regular intervals
EMOTIONAL	More likely to have healthy self-esteem
Increased moodiness/poor impulse control if they go too long without eating	More likely to have good body image
Low self-esteem	More likely to have healthy relationships
Poor body image	
Increased risk of being bullied	

FOOD ALLERGY CAUTION

As someone who has many allergies, some of which are life threatening and can cause anaphylactic shock, I am very concerned about food allergies. They can be deadly. When your child was a baby, you most likely gave one type of food at a time so you could watch for reactions. This method should continue during the toddler years. Watch for signs of food allergy:

- Rashes, hives

- Dizziness

- Swelling of the tongue, lips and face

- Stuffy or runny nose

- Wheezing and shortness of breath

- A tingling sensation on the tongue

- Abdominal cramps

- Vomiting and diarrhoea

The good news is that providing these essentials for your children doesn't have to be complicated. You don't have to weigh and measure, create a spreadsheet or buy expensive vitamins. If you provide a variety of the right whole foods in the right portions, you will be giving your children the nutrition they need. All you need to do is look at the five boxes and know that if you follow the recommended portions on page 94 and offer a variety of foods from each box over the week, you will be providing all the balanced goodness your child needs.

Some parents, when they see the carbohydrate box, ask me, 'But aren't we supposed to be limiting carbs?' Young children are different from adults. They need the energy that carbohydrates provide. The correct amounts are what counts.

DON'T SUPERSIZE IT: HEALTHY PORTIONS

Not only do we need to feed children the right kinds of food, but we need to offer it in the correct quantities. *This may be harder than it seems*: over the past twenty-five years, portion sizes have blown up so much that in one study even dietitians, people trained to understand nutrition, underestimated the calories in restaurant meals by 44 per cent. Just a few examples of how much bigger servings have become:

Then

- In 1957, the average fast-food hamburger weighed 25g.
- Twenty years ago, the average bagel was 7½ cm across.
- A serving of fries was 64g.

Now

- Today it's 175g.

- Now it's 16½ cm.

- Now it's 194g – three times bigger!

Most likely you grew up in this supersized world in which the average adult is eating 530 more calories a day than in 1970. I really urge you to get educated on healthy portion sizes so that you provide the very best for your children's long-term health and

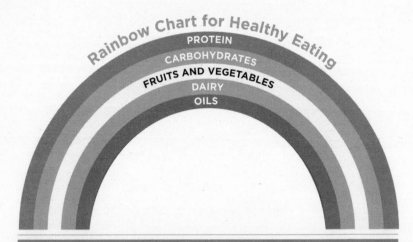

Rainbow Chart for Healthy Eating

PROTEIN
CARBOHYDRATES
FRUITS AND VEGETABLES
DAIRY
OILS

PROTEIN: chicken, eggs, turkey, seafood (sole, salmon, cod, snapper, halibut, mahi-mahi, tuna, sardines, catfish, trout, scallops, shrimp, tilapia, crab, lobster, clams), lean beef, pork, lamb, sliced meats, tofu, lentils, chickpeas, dried beans (kidney, pinto, soy, black, split peas, black-eyed peas), nut butters like peanut butter.

Protein is necessary for the proper growth of brain and body and repair of cells and tissues; it helps hold the body together (via tendons, ligaments, and bones); it is the building block of enzymes and hormones. These foods also are good sources of B vitamins, which help maintain proper energy levels, a healthy metabolism and healthy circulatory and nervous systems. Red meats and turkey are good sources of Iron, which is crucial for red blood cell and muscle development. Fish also provides essential fats.

[Note: it is recommended that fish high in mercury, such as swordfish, shark, king mackerel and tilefish, should be avoided by young children, but children can eat up to 340g a week of the varieties lower in mercury. Also, albacore tuna contains more mercury than canned light tuna, so it is recommended that young children have no more than 1 serving of albacore tuna a week.]

CARBOHYDRATES: pasta, rice, wild rice, couscous, barley, millet, crackers, bread, pitta bread, tortillas, bagels, oats, cereals. If you've been doing pretty well with eating healthy in your family and want to go to the next level, make as much as possible in this box be wholegrain and wholewheat: wholewheat bread, wholegrain tortillas, pasta, brown rice, etc.

Carbohydrates provide the body with the necessary energy to function and help the brain, heart and nervous, digestive and immune systems to function properly. They also provide fibre, which supports a healthy digestive system, help discourage overeating through being filling, and may reduce the risk of certain cancers, diabetes heart disease, and digestive disorders.

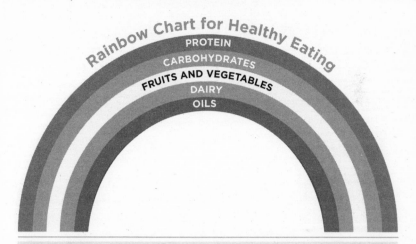

Rainbow Chart for Healthy Eating

PROTEIN
CARBOHYDRATES
FRUITS AND VEGETABLES
DAIRY
OILS

FRUITS AND VEGETABLES: fruits (apples, grapes, raspberries, blackberries, strawberries, blueberries, melons, cherries, kiwi, bananas, pineapple, oranges, peaches, plums, nectarines, mangos, papayas, prunes, dates, figs, raisins); vegetables (carrots, broccoli, peas, cabbage, lettuce, spinach, kale, chard, tomato, avocado, celery, courgettes, corn, summer squash, cucumber, sweet peppers, aubergine, onion, leeks, cauliflower, artichokes, Brussels sprouts, bok choy, mushrooms, asparagus, winter squash, green beans, potatoes, sweet potatoes, yams).

Fruits and vegetables are good sources of carbohydrates and fibre, as well as an important source of many vitamins including vitamin C, which promotes healthy muscles, connective tissue and skin.

DAIRY: milk, cheeses, yogurt, cottage cheese. Substitute soy milk, cheese, and yogurts if your child is lactose intolerant.

Dairy is a good source of vitamin D, which promotes bone and tooth formation and helps the body absorb calcium. Calcium is needed to help build strong bones as a child grows.

OILS: nuts; olive, corn, peanut, canola and nut oils.

Oils provide fats, which are critical for brain function and neurological development in early childhood, and help the absorption of certain vitamins and the production of hormones.

HEALTHY DAILY PORTIONS

Here are the latest recommendations for daily servings for
young children:

Ages 2—3

50g protein

450g dairy

225g vegetables and 225g fruit

75g carbohydrates

3 tsp oils

Ages 4—8

100g protein

550g dairy

350g vegetables and 225–350g fruit

150g carbohydrates

4 tsp oils

well-being. Don't worry about calorie counts. If you get the portion sizes right and are serving the right kinds of food, the calories take care of themselves.

Here's an easy way to figure out portions. Your child's plate should be around 15 centimetres in diameter. Fill half of the plate with fruits and vegetables, a quarter with protein and the last quarter with carbohydrates. The protein portion should be about the size of the back of your child's fist. Serve the dairy, usually a cup of milk or a yogurt, on the side. And remember – these quantities are totals for the whole day, so they include not only breakfast, lunch and dinner, but snacks as well.

MEALTIME ROUTINES

Kids need to eat at regular times. It's part of their body clock. And like with sleep, if you ignore their body clock, you will see more misbehaviour as their impulse control – not strong in little ones anyway – drops as fast as their blood sugar. The rule of thumb is that a young child needs to eat every three hours, give or take thirty minutes. That means three meals and two snacks spread throughout the day.

How to figure out the best food routine? Consistent mealtimes – breakfast, lunch and dinner – create the cornerstones. If your child eats at 7a.m., that means at 9:30 he's going to need a

KNOW HOW:
MOVE TOO!

To keep your child healthy, it's also important that you provide sixty minutes a day of physical activity. Movement not only helps with maintaining proper weight but strengthens muscles, bones and joints; helps maintain positive mood; and makes bedtime easier because your child is more likely to be tired. It also builds exercise as a healthy habit for life.

snack; lunch should be no later than 12:30, with another snack at 2:30 and dinner by 5p.m. As much as possible, have the whole family on the same mealtime routine. That way your toddler has the experience of sitting down and having meals with the family, which helps with manners and socialising, as well as with establishing lifelong good habits. Of course, that's not always possible given work and other obligations, but I encourage you to eat as a family as often as you can.

Having a mealtime routine also helps a child know when she's going to eat. It stops you from going into the pantry and feeding her too many crackers 'to tide her over'. It also prevents kids grazing all day, which is a problem because it promotes overeating.

HEALTHFUL SNACKS

Who came up with the idea that young children's snacks should only be Cheerios, crisps and pretzels? All these dry carbs don't encourage eating other food groups. You know those little snack holders with flaps that you put snacks in so kids can feed themselves? Why can't you put clementine pieces in them? Or chopped-up cucumber or grape pieces? I'm not saying that your child should never have Cheerios for a snack. But mix it up! Look at the Rainbow Chart and you'll see all kinds of ideas for healthy snacks – string cheese, half a hardboiled egg, a tube of fruit sauce, cut-up tomatoes, pieces of pineapple, a slice of turkey, baby carrots with hummus. Think about what your child is having at mealtime and give a snack that will increase variety. And remember, this is not another meal. A snack should be about the size of your child's palm.

EASY MEALS FOR BUSY PARENTS

Because I want to make feeding your child well as effortless as possible so you are not put off, I've created a week's worth of simple menus to get you started. When you look through them, you may get the idea that I don't believe in ever serving pizza, hot dogs, mac and cheese and the like. I think these are fine occasionally, but you should serve vegetables and fruit as well. And if you serve something like that for one meal, balance the week by making something more nutritious the next day.

What about convenience food like a pack of ready-made chips? Please bake, don't fry them; make sure it's just a *handful* of fries and serve a nice green vegetable too. When you serve convenience food, look at the label and the Rainbow Chart and make sure you include something from each box. A chicken casserole? That's got the carbs, protein, oils and even a few vegetables. Just put it with a piece of fruit and perhaps a salad.

I also don't want to say to never go to a fast-food restaurant. But I urge you to eat at home primarily, because you will be making healthier choices. Going out for fast food should be something you do only every now and then.

One Week's Menu Suggestions

Breakfast

1 cup milk plus:

1. Small bowl cold cereal + blueberries + yogurt
2. 1 egg, scrambled or boiled + 1 slice toast + strawberries
3. 1 cut-up chicken sausage + toast + ½ banana
4. ½ bagel + cream cheese + raspberries
5. 1 slice ham on toast + ½ orange
6. ½ tortilla rolled up with cheese + melon + yogurt
7. Small bowl oatmeal + cut-up bananas and strawberries

Lunch and Dinner

1. 1 salmon cake + carrots + rice
2. Fish pie + broccoli
3. 75g salmon + cup of pasta + peas
4. 2 fish sticks + cup couscous + veg
5. ½ breast of chicken + veg + small potato
6. Roast chicken + dumplings + veg
7. 1 meat or jam sandwich + apple + yogurt
8. 1 small homemade pizza + fruit
9. Pasta with tomato sauce and cheese + veg
10. Chicken risotto + veg
11. Ground beef + potato + peas
12. Small tuna pasta bake + veg
13. 4 meatballs + pasta + veg
14. Chicken stir-fry with veg + rice

MY SECRETS TO EATING HEALTHILY EVERY DAY

Recently I was helping a single mum with a young child learn how to eat better. She's on a limited budget, so she wasn't sure she could afford to eat fresh every day. I shared the following secrets with her and the result was that not only did she and her son eat better, but she's been saving £50 per month on her food bill!

- Start by looking in your cupboards, freezer and fridge and over time, as you run out of something, replace it with the healthy options in this chapter. You can't give your child crisps and biscuits if you don't have them.

NO-NO: SUGAR AND SALT

- *Sugar:* The **American Heart Association** recommends that sugar intake for children be no more than three teaspoons a day. My feeling is that they get all they need in fruit. Be aware that large amounts of added sugar can be hidden in bread, canned soups and vegetables, frozen dinners, cereals, ketchup and fast food.

- *Salt:* One teaspoon contains about 2,300mg of sodium. The current guideline for maximum salt intake is 1,000mg for children one to three years old and 1,200mg for children age four to six. I consider salt an unnecessary additive. Be aware that prepared foods and especially fast food often contain a large amount of sodium. Read the labels at the shop as well as the ingredients list that all chain fast-food restaurants must now provide.

- Plan a week's worth of menus using my Rainbow Chart or use the menus I provided on page 98. This only takes fifteen minutes a week. It will help you save time during the week as you try to figure out 'What shall we eat?' and will reduce children's moodiness and the impulse to head off to the nearest take-away spot.

- If you are just starting out on this healthier journey, keep the menus really simple – piece of protein, steamed veg, simple carb. As you get comfortable with the five boxes, then you can get creative and mix and match.

- See how you can stretch what you are planning on buying. For instance, one of those huge chicken breasts can serve your child for two meals. One piece can be boiled, another put into a stir-fry. A bag of rice can last for weeks.

- Make a shopping list based on your menus. Buy nothing except what is on the list. The discipline of doing this will save you money, as you won't buy impulse items. It also reduces toddler tantrums. Simply say in advance, 'If it's not on the list, we're not getting it', and then engage her in hunting for the things on the list.

- To avoid temptation in the first three weeks, stay away from the middle of the supermarket – that's where all the high-sugar, high-fat, highly processed items are shelved. The produce, dairy and proteins tend to be around the outside edges.

- Frozen is as healthy as fresh. When I see fresh fish on sale, I buy several packages and freeze some. Frozen vegetables are full of nutrients because they are picked and immediately frozen. Or you can blanch fresh vegetables such as broccoli and freeze it in serving-size containers, which will be more economical. If your fridge looks colourful, you're on the right track.

- Cook meals on the weekends, put them into serving-size containers, then freeze or refrigerate. That way you don't even have to think about what to serve during the week, so you don't get caught short and go out for fast food. When I was a kid, there was always a dish in the fridge with salad in it and it's what my father still does when I go to visit.

As a busy parent, do your best to stick to the meal plan and the foods that you've bought. If you fall off track, don't do the 'Oh well, I'll start again on Monday' thing. Get back on it the very next meal. Then look at why you didn't stick to your plan. Be honest with yourself. Were you tired and had planned something too difficult? Did you not want to deal with your child's behaviour if you said no to something unhealthy? Were you late and your kids were screaming from hunger? Understanding why you made the choice you did can help you put healthful solutions in place – for example, have emergency meals ready to go, make your menus even simpler, or just take a deep breath and decide to deal with your child's complaining tonight. You can do it; it just takes discipline. You are in control of the choices you make.

'I'VE COOKED IT, BUT WILL THEY EAT IT?'

One of the obstacles parents face when deciding to serve more healthy food is worrying that their children won't eat it. It's easy for parents to lose the enthusiasm to cook healthily because they put effort in and then their child says he doesn't like it. So it's tempting to serve chicken fingers and carrot sticks every day because you know he'll eat them and you don't want to waste food.

In these circumstances, you need to remember what your purpose really is. It's not to get approval from your child, but to make sure she gets the nutrition she needs. It's very easy for young children to get fixated on certain foods. It's like their wanting you to read the same book over and over again. It's familiar, so they like it. When it comes to food, it's up to you to help them expand beyond the familiar.

When parents say to me, 'My kids will only eat noodles', or 'All they'll eat is cheese', I respond, 'Your kids will only eat what you keep serving them!' I looked after kids for seventeen years before I started helping families on television and I never had a picky eater. That's not a coincidence.

Parents *create* picky eaters because they worry their child will starve unless they give them only what they ask for. In the next chapter, I'll show you step by step how to deal with picky eating and other problematic food behaviours.

To help your child learn to eat a wide variety of foods, be sure to sit down and eat with him. I once helped a family on TV with twin girls who were very naughty and brought that behaviour to the table. Yes, the mum needed to eliminate their naughty behaviour. But part of the problem was that she wasn't sitting and eating with them. She'd lean up against the sink – away from the food she'd served – because she was worried about her weight. I taught her to sit with them and eat something. This encouraged the twins not only to eat but also to behave better because they weren't so bored. Don't rub your poor eating habits off onto your kids.

THE LITTLE CHEF TECHNIQUE

Get your little one involved in preparing the meal and setting the table. I call this my 'Little Chef' technique. The key is to make the task something he can do – appropriate for his age. Your two-year-old can help with measuring or pouring. Your three- and four-year-old can help stir or mix. And an almost-five-year-old can help you to come up with the menu and get involved in the cooking or setting the table. Use lots of encouragement and praise for each task he completes.

SEVEN

Food SOS

Making sure your children eat properly is not just a matter of serving a variety of healthy food in the right portions. They actually have to eat what you serve. Because of the push for independence that happens during these ages, mealtimes can become a power play. Your child is most likely pushing back not because she truly doesn't like what you are serving but because she's at the stage where she pushes back on everything and food – what she puts in her mouth – is one thing she feels she can control.

With eating, a destructive cycle can all too easily get set up – she does something and then you react in a certain way, then she reacts to your reaction and it goes round and round. Your child is never going to change on her own. That means you have to change your behaviour so that hers will change in response.

It's easy for parents to be reactive around eating because it's an emotionally loaded issue. Humans have an inborn instinct to feed their young, the same as all other animals. When a child refuses to eat something – or most things – parents unconsciously get frightened. They know their child needs to eat, so they give in, thereby creating picky eating, grazing and other bad habits around food.

That's why the SOS approach is so important here, especially the Step Back. It helps you not become distraught that your child doesn't want to eat things you know are good for him or is refusing to eat at all. With emotional detachment, your logic can kick in and you realise that he's not going to wither away under the chair this very moment. Then, in the Observe phase, you can look calmly at what you've been doing to create this situation as well as exactly how your child has been behaving.

When you Step In, be prepared to come in with patience, calmness and the willingness to put in place what you need to in order to get past the problem. You absolutely can't let your feelings show. Is it frustrating for me to sit at the table for an hour with a child to deal with an eating issue? Of course it is! Does the child know? No way. I know showing frustration will only make matters worse. Instead I show patience, tolerance and commitment because I want resolution. That's where being disciplined comes in. You commit to doing what you need to in order to turn the situation around.

Of course, food refusal is not the only hot-button food issue. In this chapter, you'll also get my advice on staying at the table, spitting out or dropping food, manners and other mealtime problems.

REFUSING TO EAT A VARIETY OF FOOD

Your three-year-old son refuses to eat anything but breaded chicken strips and carrot sticks. When he was younger, he would eat anything, but for the past three months he won't even try a bite of anything else.

Step Back: Take a breath and don't react.

Observe: This is a situation where you need to ask yourself some tough questions. Do you understand the importance of your child eating a variety of protein, carbs, fruits, vegetables, dairy and fats throughout the week and the quantities he should be eating? How many times a week do you create balanced meals? How many times do you offer your child a choice of eating something else and he says no, so you give him chicken strips and carrots? How many times have you served something else and stuck to your guns, telling him, 'That's the only thing you're getting to eat', then when he's refused to eat it, you've taken the plate away – and later given him something he wanted from the pantry? How many times have you felt upset and didn't want to persevere, so you just gave in?

What do you want to achieve? Your child eating well-rounded meals with appropriate variety throughout the week.

Step In: You're the one who has been serving him chicken strips and carrots every day. So your game plan is to do the *complete opposite* of everything you discovered you've been doing. In Chapter 6, you learned about what he should be eating and in what portions. Now you're going to create balanced meals for him and you are not going to ask, 'Do you want this?' Rather, you are going to tell him nicely that this is what he's going to be eating and persevere with it. Stipulate how much he has to eat and praise him for doing it. Let him know how pleased you are. If he starts to resist, remind him that when he eats a couple of bites of each, he can get down to play. Rather than making a big deal out of the fact that he 'must' eat something, encourage him by telling him that once he eats, he can move on to something much more fun.

And last but not least, if he refuses to eat, *do not give him anything else* – and I mean *anything*! Even if his bottom lip is drooping and his face looks so sad. If he knows you will give him something later from the pantry, of course he won't eat what's in front of him. Missing one meal is not going to harm him.

REJECTING VEGETABLES

You know the importance of your two-and-a-half-year-old eating vegetables. But a lot of what you serve he says he doesn't like. Just this week, he rejected tomatoes, peppers, cauliflower and cabbage. You've heard that children often don't like vegetables and you're afraid if it keeps going like this, he'll end up not eating any.

Step Back: Take a breath and don't react.

Observe: How many times have you served a particular vegetable? How many different ways have you cooked it? Are you mixing it into other things? Serving it raw as well as cooked?

When he says he doesn't like it, are you giving in and giving him something else because it's easier? Once he says he doesn't like it, do you never serve it again?

What do you want to achieve? Your child eating a wide range of vegetables.

Step In: When young children say, 'I don't like this', parents think that means always, forever and in any form whatsoever. What they really mean is 'I don't want to eat this', which can be for a number of reasons: they don't want to eat it *today*; they don't like it in that particular form; they're hoping you'll ask them what they do want to eat and give that to them; they want to get down and play. Plus children this age are very fickle – one day they love apples and the next week they'll tell you they hate them.

You have to believe me when I tell you that it takes at least twelve or fifteen times of consistently eating a certain food in a variety of forms for a child to establish a true dislike. At this stage it's about helping him develop his palate, which generally doesn't fully happen until he's around five. Then when he says he doesn't like something, it's most likely a true dislike, particularly if it's a few things, not every vegetable.

I'm concerned that parents expect problems with vegetables. I think a lot of it is created by the media – they say there's a problem, so now you expect a problem. If you simply expect him to eat vegetables, then it tends not to become an issue.

To help him develop a taste for different kinds of vegetables, experiment with serving them in different forms. You'll discover that he likes some vegetables mixed in with other food. Chop them up finely and mix them in with rice or pasta or sauce, for instance. Start off with root vegetables – swede, carrots and sweet potatoes – and mix other root vegetables in with those. Make a stew that mixes veggies with meat. Some he may prefer raw and others cooked. And don't take a vegetable totally off your list. Try it again in another form in a couple of weeks.

When you serve a vegetable, treat it casually – don't focus on the vegetable. You don't want to set up a battle of wills. Tell him he needs to eat his meal and then he can get down and do something fun. If he resists, here are my tips:

- Don't replace the problem food with another one.
- Compromise – have him eat a certain amount of it, but only negotiate once.
- Talk about something else.
- The average meal for a toddler takes about thirty minutes. If you are there for more than forty minutes total, he can get down. But do not give him anything else to eat until the next mealtime.

ACTING UP AT DINNERTIME

You have a two-and-a-half-year-old and a four-year-old. You pick them up from day care and get home around six. By the time dinner is on the table, it's nearly seven. Dinner doesn't usually go well, as there tends to be lots of whining and acting up. Forget about teaching manners and conversation – you're just trying to get through the meal without a blowout. Often you end up yelling.

Step Back: Take a breath and don't react.

Observe: What time are your kids getting up in the morning and when are they going to sleep? When are they having lunch and snacks?

What do you want to achieve? A peaceful dinnertime where you enjoy being together.

Step In: It seems you are trying to have an enjoyable dinner with cranky, tired children. They're eating too late, which means most likely they're not getting enough sleep either and that is causing problems at the end of the day. As I wrote earlier, the body clock for a young child works on about a twelve-hour cycle – up for twelve hours and sleeping for twelve hours, with a need to eat every three hours, give or take thirty minutes. When parents mess with that to fit their own schedule, it often creates behaviour problems at the dinner table.

Is it possible to get home earlier? Or to have prepared food in advance so that you eat as soon as you come home? Or to serve them part of their dinner in the car if you have a longish drive and perhaps only fruit and a yogurt at the table, so they have the experience of eating with you when their blood sugar isn't so low? Make sure that the afternoon snack at day care is substantial so that they don't come in the door starving.

WON'T STAY AT THE TABLE

Your three-year-old takes a few bites of food and then gets down from the table and wants to play. You're concerned she is not getting enough food at mealtimes.

Step Back: Take a breath and don't react.

Observe: How long are you expecting her to sit? Have you worked on her listening skills and attention span? Can she sit and focus on a puzzle or game? Have you taught her that she must stay at the table until she is excused? Do you let her graze later to 'make up' for eating poorly at the table? Do you sit down at the table with her so that she understands this is what we do when we eat?

What do you want to achieve? Her staying at the table until she eats the proper amount and is excused.

Step In: Problems with staying at the table are resolved by first recognising a realistic time that children should be sitting there, which at this age is no longer than thirty minutes. So if your child sits down for two minutes and then wants to get up, you need to work on expanding her attention. (See Chapter 10.) My niece is two years old and she can actually sit down at a table with all of us for an hour! She can do that because the early learning ground-work has been done on her concentration skills.

In addition to working on attention span, you need to make your expectation clear about staying at the table: 'You need to sit here and eat until Mummy or Daddy says you can be excused.' Teach her how to ask to get down: 'Say, "May I be excused, please?"' Try the Stay at Table technique with a three- or four-year-old (see next page). Don't reward her for not eating by letting her graze later. If she doesn't eat the amount you've decided she should, don't give her any food until the next mealtime. And make sure you are a good role model for sitting at the table by having regular mealtimes when you all sit together.

THE STAY AT TABLE TECHNIQUE

1. Set a timer for ten minutes and challenge him to sit at the table until the buzzer goes off.
2. Each day, set the timer for an extra couple of minutes. Make sure you build his attention span during the day as well.
3. Within several days, your child should have no problem sitting at the table for twenty to thirty minutes during every mealtime.

SPITS OUT FOOD

Your twenty-month-old is spitting out her meat. You can't tell if she doesn't like it, is playing around, or is doing it defiantly.

Step Back: Take a breath and don't react.

Observe: What kind of meat is she spitting out? How has it been cooked? How small are you cutting it? Does she do it if it's mixed in with other food? How does she do with raw vegetables? Also, how is her speech? Does she talk much? Do you understand what she is saying? Does she have most of her teeth in?

What do you want to achieve? Her eating food properly.

Step In: At this age, a child has already made the transition from eating lumpy or mushy food to whole pieces of meat and vegetables. She's literally learning how to chew. Some kids get lazy. That's why you often see spitting out food, particularly meat, at this age – youngsters get lazy and suck the juice out of the meat, then spit the fibres out. As a rule of thumb, red meat is always slightly tougher than fish or poultry, so at the beginning it's easier to serve the softer proteins. When you do serve red meat, start with braises and casseroles so the meat is very tender. Make sure the pieces are very small so that they are easy to chew and swallow. The same goes for raw vegetables – make sure the pieces are small. She'll get the hang of it and the spitting out will stop. In the meantime, understand that she's not being defiant, she's just learning.

You might be wondering why I am asking you to think about speech. It's because I have seen a correlation between speech development and the ability to chew well. Both require strong facial muscles and chewing also promotes the development of more saliva, which helps with talking. So if you notice any speech issues, I would work on auditory development as well as deal with chewing. One supports the other.

NOT EATING ENOUGH

Your four-year-old eats like a bird at mealtimes. It's not that he doesn't like certain types of food but that he won't eat much of anything. You're afraid he's not eating enough, so you try to make sure he gets plenty of milk, for the protein. You don't want to force him to eat, but you don't think he's getting the proper nutrition. Given that he's not eating a lot, you're not sure how long you should keep him at the table.

Step Back: Take a breath and don't react.

Observe: When are his mealtimes? Snack times? How big are the snacks? How much milk are you giving him? Is he having more carbs than protein, fruits and vegetables?

What do you want to achieve? His eating the proper amounts of the right foods at the right times of the day.

Step In: Look at the overall picture of what and how much he is eating daily and compare it to the recommended quantities on page 94. In order to up the quantity of food at mealtimes, I suggest that you eliminate snacks for a while and keep the quantity of milk down so he doesn't fill up on milk. The recommended dairy portion for a four- to eight-year-old is 550g a day, which includes milk, yogurt and the equivalent amount of cheese. Then start to build up the amount of food that he's eating at meals. Make sure you have regular mealtimes and prepare balanced meals.

Help him learn that mealtimes are for eating by encouraging him to eat, rather than carrying on a conversation with him. When a toddler sits down to eat, you've probably got a concentrated eating time of ten minutes. That's when he needs to be really focused on eating. Then there's another ten to fifteen minutes of encouragement to finish off the rest, taking his plate away and eating perhaps a yogurt and some fruit for dessert.

CHOKING AND GAGGING AT MEALS

Your two-and-a-half-year-old daughter has started choking and gagging at meals. You've been to the doctor, who says there is no medical problem. You're careful about giving her small portions, but that doesn't seem to help. It's very frightening. This has been going on for months. You now have a young baby who needs to eat as well, so you feel even more pressured to resolve this issue.

Step Back: Take a breath and don't react.

Observe: When does this happen? With all food? Or only things she doesn't like? When she eats with a spoon but not with finger foods? When she gags and chokes, how do you respond? Do you get upset? Take the food away? Let her get down and give her a snack soon after?

What do you want to achieve? Her learning that gagging and choking will not prevent her from eating healthy meals.

Step In: Believe it or not, this situation is not uncommon. Since you've ruled out a medical problem, it's almost always an attempt to avoid eating something she doesn't want to eat and/or to get a rise out of you. Choking is the last trick in the bag; it leads to a gag spasm, which leads to perhaps a spot of vomiting, which leads to the parent taking the food away. I've seen this happen and then ten minutes later the same child asks for a yogurt, gets it and has absolutely no trouble eating it.

To change this dynamic, understand that it is a manipulation. You must stay calm and not let your face show disgust or fear that something terrible is going to happen to her. (See box on page 117 for the difference between true and fake choking and how to do the Heimlich manoeuvre if necessary.)

Feed your baby before your toddler so you won't be feeling pressured. Then sit down with your toddler, give her a very small portion and encourage her to eat. Don't pay any attention to gagging or vomiting. If she gags, encourage her to chew. If she vomits, calmly clean it up and have her finish the rest of the food before getting down. Give hugs and praise for every bite swallowed. Over time, the behaviour will go away.

EATING WITH UTENSILS

Your daughter is eighteen months old and still eating with her fingers. Sometimes you feed her with a spoon, but she won't do it herself. You don't know whether to try something else or just wait till she's a bit older. Now that you think about it, you're not sure at what age it's appropriate for her to start using a knife and fork either.

Step Back: Take a breath and don't react.

Observe: What kinds of things are you giving her to eat? Can they all be eaten with the fingers? Have you shown her how to eat with a spoon? How is her hand-eye coordination? Are you working on her fine motor skills by having her do puzzles with knobs and threading large beads? What kind of spoon have you given her?

What do you want to achieve? Her ability to feed herself, starting with a spoon and moving up when appropriate to a knife and fork.

Step In: An eighteen-month-old is definitely old enough to be feeding herself with a spoon. To help her learn, put your hand over hers and guide the spoon into her mouth. Stop serving food

KNOW HOW: IS SHE REALLY CHOKING OR ACTING UP?

True choking can be deadly. So it's important to be able to tell the difference between real and faked. With fake choking, it's sporadic. There's gagging, but she carries on chewing and looks at you for a reaction – and cries while she's at it, to really tug on your heartstrings. Whereas when a child really is choking, there's no room for anything else. All there is is choking and a look of desperation in her eyes. It's continuous. In that case, you want to perform the Heimlich manoeuvre:

1. Have someone call 999 while you stand or kneel behind your child with your arms around her waist. (If she's unconscious, lay her on her back and kneel at her feet.)

2. Make a fist and hold it with your other hand against her abdomen, just above the navel and below the rib cage. (If your child is down, place the heel of your hand in the middle of her stomach just above the belly button and below the rib cage, resting your other hand on top of the first.) Pressing firmly but gently on her abdomen, give upward thrusts in sets of five until the object is expelled.

3. If the object isn't cleared and your child loses consciousness, lay her on her back and open her mouth. If you see the obstruction, carefully sweep your index finger across the back of her throat to remove it.

4. Perform rescue breathing: Open the airway by tilting the head back and lifting the chin up.

5. Keeping the airway open, pinch your child's nose shut with your fingers, seal your mouth over hers, and give

two slow breaths. Continue mouth-to-mouth respiration until she resumes normal breathing or medical help arrives. Note: If your child's chest doesn't begin to rise, the object is still blocking her airway. Repeat steps 1 to 5 until the object is coughed up or help arrives.

6. After a choking incident that requires the Heimlich manoeuvre, take your child to the doctor to make sure everything is okay, even if she seems fine.

that can be easily picked up by fingers and move to lumpy rice and vegetable dishes that must be eaten with a spoon.

The right size spoon helps too. Sometimes parents still give their kids baby spoons, which are so small they can't get enough food per spoonful. The right spoon for this age should be a teaspoon.

Because of a lack of dexterity, she won't be able to use a fork properly until about three and a knife until about five – and even then you will have to help. You can help her develop that dexterity through the hand-eye coordination games I recommend in Chapter 10 and by having her pick up small items with her fingers, such as cut-up bits of fruit.

Once she's ready for a fork, beware of the plastic ones that can't spear anything. There are brands making such forks for 'child safety'. I've tried to get a piece of chicken on that type of fork and couldn't do it for love or money because it was too pliant. Children get frustrated and end up using these forks like a spoon and then food falls through the grooves. I don't see any reason not to use a small stainless-steel fork when the time comes.

By five, if you've been helping her both with the right early learning activities and putting your hands over hers and doing it together, what I call shadowing, she should be able to use a knife and a fork – not necessarily correctly, but she should be able to use them. You'll have to cut the harder food up and shadow her at the beginning. To prepare, when she gets a bit older, you can have her cut Play-Doh with the knives that come in the set.

KNOW HOW: SELF-FEEDING

Being able to use utensils is a seven-step process from infancy to age five:

1. You feed.

2. He eats with his fingers.

3. Both of you hold the spoon.

4. He eats with a spoon by himself.

5. You help him use a fork.

6. He uses a fork by himself.

7. You help him use a knife.

TEACHING GOOD TABLE MANNERS

You recently went out to dinner with friends who have children the same age as yours (three and four) and noticed how much better behaved they were at the table than your kids. They said 'please' and 'thank you' and asked to be excused. You're not quite

sure why they have better manners than your children, but it was
a wake-up call for you to do something.

Step Back: Take a breath and don't react.

Observe: What have you done to teach your children proper manners? Do you tell them what to say and do? Do you have good manners yourself? Are you eating together for at least one meal a day so that they get to watch and learn from you?

What do you want to achieve? To make sure your children are
well-mannered.

Step In: I'm a stickler for manners, which is one of the reasons I believe in having meals together as much as possible. As I've said before, a lot is taught through children mimicking you. They watch *you* with your knife and fork and then *they* want to use a knife and fork. If you burp at the table and say 'excuse me', they'll be more likely to say 'excuse me' when they burp. If you use your napkin, they'll begin to use it too. That's why you need to be a role model for good manners. Set the standard – have good manners yourself.

Manners also have to be taught through instruction, prompting and lots and lots of repetition. This is one area where you can definitely feel like a broken record: 'What do you say when someone hands you something?' 'Thank you'. Manners have to be prompted until they become automatic. If you are disciplined about prompting and repeating, in a few years your children will have beautiful manners at home and out in the world without your needing to say anything.

KNOW HOW:
TABLE MANNERS

By the age of four, all children should know the following:

- How to use a spoon and fork

- How to ask to pass something rather than grabbing: 'May I please have the . . .'

- To put a napkin on their lap and wipe their mouth with it

- Chew with mouth closed

- Say 'please' when making a request and 'thank you' when receiving something

- Say 'May I be excused please' when leaving the table

To know what you should be teaching, see the box above. Young children also often need instruction on what size bites are appropriate and how to chew and swallow before taking another bite.

Break down the table skills. When they are tiny, you can teach them to say, 'Down, please'. As they get older and their vocabulary gets better, they can graduate to 'Please may I get down from the table?' If he's using his sleeve instead of his napkin, tuck the napkin into his shirt like a bib till he learns to use it. Then it can move to his lap.

EIGHT

Social Rules

Every parent knows what it feels like when your children have been sick and you've been cooped up in the house for days. The kids are starting to feel better and now they're running laps around the living room and you're all going stir-crazy. That's when it's most obvious that it's important to break up your day at home and get out with your children for some fresh air, a change of scenery and a chance to run around and do something different.

Part of raising toddlers is getting them out to enjoy the activities that are available where you live: library reading time, church playtimes, Mummy and Me music or dance or swimming classes, parks, playgrounds, playdates and play groups and so on. You want your children to socialise with children of their own age. To get exercise. To get exposure to new people, places and experiences.

When you go out with your kids, whether around the block or across the country, they get to see the world, to experience the beauty of nature and the seasons. They have the opportunity to explore, which provokes questions about life. They can understand what a bus is, not from reading a book but from riding it. They see how other people behave and learn how to interact in various places. Through these experiences, you start to make deposits into your child's memory bank and build up family memories too – whether it's something big like a family vacation or just a picnic in the park.

Going out is good for you too. If you are a stay-at-home parent, you *need* – and I use the word *need* on purpose – to get out and have healthy conversations with other adults so that you're not continuously using children's language and living in what I call Mary Poppins Land. And all parents should be able to run errands with their young children without major battles and have fun together at social occasions, such as a cousin's wedding or a neighbour's barbecue. When you know how to do it, it can be absolutely delightful to shop with your child, to take him to the little farm to see a real horse, to enjoy a swim class together, to take a family trip.

OVERCOMING THE OBSTACLES

Going out and about often presents a real lot of issues for parents, both in making sure children know how to behave in public and in terms of safety so that both you and your kids can enjoy the experience.

Effects on Children of Not Getting Out Regularly	Effects on Children of Getting Out Regularly
PHYSICAL	**PHYSICAL**
More likely to be rambunctious, full of pent-up energy	Less likely to be rambunctious at home
May be more aggressive and destructive	Less likely to be aggressive and destructive
Less likely to be fit due to lack of exercise; may be less coordinated	More likely to be physically fit and coordinated
SOCIAL	**SOCIAL**
Uncomfortable with new people and places, greater separation anxiety	Comfortable with new people and places, less separation anxiety
Less adaptable to the environment	More adaptable to the environment
More likely to misbehave in public	Less likely to misbehave in public
Less able to share space and toys	More able to share space and toys
Less prepared to go to school and be in a group	More prepared to go to school and be in a group
INTELLECTUAL	**INTELLECTUAL**
Less understanding of how the world works	More understanding of how the world works
May have impaired academic achievement due to lack of enough stimulation	Likely to do well in school, learn from teamwork with others

At the root of parents' fear of being out in public is that they are worried they won't be able to maintain appropriate behaviour from their child and then will be made to feel embarrassed or ashamed by the adults around them. We've all heard the horror stories of pilots turning planes around because of a child's misbehaviour.

It's a vicious cycle – parents' inability to resolve an issue with their toddler in public has led to less tolerance and compassion from people, which results in parents not wanting to get themselves in that situation. That's why I want to make sure you have the rules in place that will allow you and your child to enjoy the wide world outside your door. I also offer you my suggestions for fun daily activities and my tried-and-true Jo-Jo tips for trips short and long. It is my hope that when you put these rules, tips and techniques in place, not only will you enjoy daily activities together, but you'll feel much more confident and excited about taking longer trips with your little one – whether by car, plane or train.

Here again, going out for socialisation is interrelated with the other four rules. If you haven't got behaviour under control at home, you're going to see that bad behaviour when you go out as well. If you haven't worked on the early learning skills, your child isn't going to have the attention span to enjoy things such as library time or gymnastics classes. And if you don't have healthy patterns of eating and sleeping in place, your child won't have the emotional and physical resilience to enjoy the experiences you're creating for him and you'll have to deal with more tantrums.

It works the other way as well – when you put the fundamentals of social and safety skills in place and expose your child to these activities, you are increasing his learning, his ability to get along with others and his good behaviour in public. His brain wires up through the experiences he has and so the greater the variety of experiences you provide, the more he will be stimulated. Sitting down and doing a puzzle is learning, but so is going to the store and identifying which vegetable is broccoli. I'm a firm believer that when something's fun, children learn quicker because it's enjoyable. And they remember better because it comes from a good experience.

Here's an example of how these things relate. I once helped a family on TV that had a young boy. When we went to the park, he ran off, not listening, out of the park gate.

Yes, this boy needed to be taught traffic safety. But the bigger issue was that he didn't listen to his parents about anything. I first needed to teach them how to communicate with their child so that he would take them seriously. Until they put the behaviour basics in place, they could never trust him to stay with them in public.

So in addition to having the other four rules in place, what a disciplined parent needs to do in order to happily go out in public falls into two categories: safety and social skills.

SAFETY FIRST

When a child becomes mobile, parents are faced with a dilemma: it's easier for you to keep him strapped into his buggy because you can control him more easily, but he wants to get out and move – and he should! Walking is good exercise and exercise is important for kids of all ages. Not only will it help with his gross motor skills (legs and arms), but study after study have shown that fit children do better in school because exercise enhances cognitive ability. Plus you don't want to be pushing him around in a buggy at age four!

Learning how to walk safely is a crucial skill young children should be practising from a very young age. They won't be totally trustworthy until they are older. But remember, kids learn through repetition, so it's never too early to start. Here are the rules you should be teaching each time you are out:

* Any time you are near a road or crossing a street, she must hold your hand.
* Always walk on the pavement if there is one.
* When you come to a kerb, practise what to do: 'Stop and look both ways.'
* Practise what to do at stoplights: 'Red means we have to stop. When the man appears green, we can go.'
* As your child gets older, you can make it a game: 'What does a red light mean?' 'What's the number one rule about crossing streets?' (Stop and look both ways.)

In addition to practising at crosswalks while holding hands, you want to help your child learn how to walk near you on pavements without worrying that she will run away from you or dart into traffic. That's why I developed my Roaming technique (see below). It allows you to begin to teach your toddler independence in public while making sure she is safe. Start with Part I when she's around two. It requires that she hold on to the buggy at all times. Use Part II for a child between three and five. This gives her a bit of space while building up your confidence that she will listen to you and not run off. Of course, since young children can be impulsive, make sure that she's never so far that you can't grab her if necessary. And whenever you walk, your child should be on the inside of the kerb and you on the outside for that added layer of protection.

The more kids you have, the more it's crucial to put this in place. Break it into small steps if need be. I once helped a family in Arizona who had triplets and a new baby. The biggest thing for the mother was to feel that she could get out of the house every day. Otherwise, she'd have cabin fever with four kids under the age of five. I taught her the Roaming technique with all three of her boys and the baby in the buggy. We did a mock run of it with a doll in the pram first, so that she would get it down with the triplets first without having to worry about the baby. We tried it in her cul-de-sac first and then in the park. Once she got the hang of it, we put the real baby in the buggy.

THE ROAMING TECHNIQUE, PART I

1. Between eighteen months and two years, when he wants to walk, give a clear choice between two options: hold your hand and walk or hold on to the buggy. What he can't do is walk freely by himself.

2. If he refuses to listen and make a choice, then he has to be in the buggy.

3. Put him in for fifteen minutes, then give him another chance to try again. Please remember you are training him to be safe and independent while walking beside you.

4. Always hold your hand over theirs as you are walking.

THE ROAMING TECHNIQUE, PART II

Use the Roaming technique, part II, for children between three and five years:

1. Practise in a quiet, car-free place, such as a park or a garden. It is vital to have a safe environment while he learns this rule.

2. Explain that you are going to let him out of the buggy, but when you say 'Stop' and hold up your hand, he needs to stop. Your child should be just at the front wheel of the buggy.

3. The first few times have him beside you and then say 'Stop' and hold up your hand. If he doesn't stop, you will have him hold your hand or the buggy for several minutes. If he does wait for you, praise him. Then let him go again, but always in front, not behind you so that you may look out for danger.

4. When you say 'Stop', use an authoritative tone of voice.

5. Work up to allowing him to go a little bit further ahead. Let him know that Mummy or Daddy always need to see him – which doesn't mean twenty yards in front of

you. (Remember, this teaching can only be done in a park or somewhere that is car-free.)

6. As you build up trust and he shows he can listen, let him walk further ahead within reason. Remember, trust is built on an invisible child leash. So don't forget you must pull that leash in when you are on a busy street. In a park you can have a little more leeway.

Remember, you can never relax your vigilance even if you've trained your child well. I was reminded of this the other day when I was at a nearby shopping centre. Standing at the top of a down escalator was a tiny little girl, three at the most. I looked around for an adult but saw no one. Meanwhile, the little girl was edging closer to the escalator. I was on high alert because she could have tumbled down the escalator and seriously injured herself. So I decided to lead her away from the escalator. As I did, her mother came along. She'd been talking to a friend and the girl had wandered off. Fortunately, nothing fatal happened. But of course, if you're going to have a conversation, you need to keep your child in front of you and near at all times. She can disappear in the blink of an eye.

PUTTING SOCIAL SKILLS IN PLACE

In order for your child to go out and enjoy playdates and play groups, parks and playgrounds, activity centres and so on, she needs to be comfortable mingling with other children and have an ability to share space and toys. A child first learns about respect and etiquette at home. But these things have to be consistently reinforced. When you expose your child to social situations outside of home, it gives her that many more opportunities to practise waiting, sharing, taking turns and treating other people's things with respect.

Parents must explicitly teach these skills. Parents often tell toddlers, 'You need to share' or 'You have to take turns', without teaching them what that actually means. That's why I developed the Taking Turns and Time Sharing techniques. (See page 132.) I strongly suggest you do both on a regular basis with your child. It's much easier for a little one to learn with a parent than in the heat of the moment with another toddler. Then, when you are in a social situation, you can remind him what you've been practising.

Sharing is a concept that children learn over time, with a lot of prompting and practice. Don't feel bad if you sound like a broken record. He'll eventually get it. If you start at around two and a half – before that, a child's attention span is so short that 'waiting your turn' doesn't make sense – then by the time he's three he should understand the concept, even if he may not always do it perfectly.

When kids play together, I like to do what I call forced sharing, which is when I purposely give them something they have to share – paper and one box of crayons, or one box of Lego, or one set of sand toys in the park. Having only one set of something really encourages cooperation and primes a child for school, where she must share resources. Yes, you absolutely will have to mediate squabbles – children at this age can't do this on their own

– but your child will be learning important social skills.

Toddlers can become territorial about space as well as objects. They want to be the only person on the slide or in the ball pen or in the playhouse. Sharing space must also be taught – that these are spaces for everyone and he must let anyone who wants to use it.

THE TAKING TURNS TECHNIQUE

1. Do it as a game. 'Your turn': give the picture or whatever you're playing with to your child. 'Now my turn': you do the colouring.
2. He'll see the switch back and forth and how he has to wait until it's his turn. Eventually he will be able to do it with friends.

THE TIME SHARING TECHNIQUE

1. Have one toy and tell her you're going to share.
2. Show her a timer and explains that until it pings, she will play with the toy.
3. Give her the toy and set the timer for five minutes.
4. When it pings, reset the timer for five minutes. Then you play with the toy.
5. Switch again when the timer goes off. This enables her to see that the time she has to wait is not endless and she will get the toy back, which allows her to relax and share. This builds trust too.
6. Increase the time as she gets the idea.

Successful Playdates and Play Groups

Playdates and play groups are wonderful opportunities for toddlers to develop social skills. Here are my tips for successful get-togethers:

- Don't stay too long – 90 to 120 minutes is good.
- Mornings or afternoons after naps are best.
- Do a couple of planned activities, such as colouring or Lego and have some unstructured time as well.
- Children this age need to be supervised in terms of behaviour and helped to figure out what to do. You will most likely see parallel play in two- and three-year-olds (playing alongside but not with one another). As your child reaches four and five, you will see greater interaction develop.
- If it's a play group, participating parents should agree on the rules and that each parent will discipline their own child. Keep the rules very simple – for instance, no hitting, biting, spitting or grabbing toys. Explain the rules to the children and explain that if someone doesn't follow the rules, he will have to sit out. (See the Sideline technique, page 221.)
- If it's a playdate and the other parent isn't with you, I like to get the other parent's permission to discipline her child – and make sure to tell the parent about it when she comes back if you've had to. When you are in agreement about caring for the kids, it's a win-win.

Great Daily Activities

Short classes aimed at this age – music, dance, gymnastics, swimming, cooking, etc. – are great both for the brain stimulation they provide and for exposure to other children and some of the rules your child will encounter in school, such as standing in line, waiting your turn, listening to the instructor and following directions. But not everyone can afford these classes and some parents don't have schedules that accommodate regular attendance. Fortunately, there are all kinds of free or low-cost activities you can do with your child. Here's a list of some of my favourites, along with the benefits they offer:

- Visiting a play centre (exercise, gross motor development, social skills, development of imagination through creative play).
- Attending library or bookshop story time (language development, pre-reading skills, concentration, attention span, social skills).
- Visiting farms, zoos, petting zoos and aquariums (exercise, gross motor development, exposure to nature, language development).
- Exploring the edge of a pond, stream, or lake (exercise, visual observation, exposure to nature). *Warning: young children can drown in 1½ centimetres of water. Make sure you never leave his side or turn your back on him, even for a second.*
- Walking in parks, gathering pebbles to paint at home (exercise, gross and fine motor development, visual

observation, exposure to nature).

- Going to interactive children's museums (fine motor development, critical thinking skills, understanding of how things work).
- Doing a nature scavenger hunt (exercise, gross and fine motor development, visual observation, exposure to nature).
- Going on a short train or boat ride (language development, understanding of how things work).
- Attending a farmers' market (social skills, language development).
- Visiting an airport, fire station, or construction site (language development, understanding of how things work).

Doing Errands Happily

Parents tell me all the time that they avoid doing errands with their toddler because they don't want the hassle. Plus there's nothing more embarrassing than a public tantrum. (See Part 3!)

There's no question that shopping with a toddler adds a level of challenge to the experience, but that doesn't mean you should avoid it. Otherwise you are depriving your child of exposure to the outside world, as well as the opportunity to teach him that he can't have everything he sees. Here are my top tips for making errands enjoyable and as tantrum-free as possible:

- Look at your week and spread the errands out. That way you won't have to be trying to get him back into the car seat for the fifth time in a morning.

- Spend no more than thirty to sixty minutes on 'your' things, then do some activity he enjoys – park, activity centre, etc. Keeping it short will prevent tantrums.

- Go right after breakfast or an afternoon nap and snack so he's not tired or hungry. Tantrums and naughty behaviour are more likely if you bump up against meal or sleep times.

- Have a bottle of water and a non-perishable snack in the car to give him if necessary.

- Give him something to do in the shop by using the Involvement technique (see below). Have him name the fruits and vegetables. Let him put the cereal in the trolley. If you can keep him interested by interacting with him, he will most likely be cooperative.

THE INVOLVEMENT TECHNIQUE

1. As you go through a shop, talk about items on your list. Ask her to help you find them. Have her feel the different textures, smell the different scents, identify the different colours and names of items.

2. Give her a crayon and have her tick off each item on your list as you go.

3. Give descriptive praise for what she gets right and inform her about what she doesn't remember.

4. The more you do with her, the better she will get.

Avoiding Shop Scenes

Parents get into trouble doing errands with young children be-cause they don't set up expectations in advance and aren't clear in their communication. They tend to fall into two categories:

The Indecisive Parent

Your child asks, 'Can I have this, Daddy?' You respond, 'Ummmm, I don't know. Let me think about it. Maybe.' Now he believes you've said yes because you didn't say no and he is disap-pointed, if not angry, when you get to the checkout stand and say no. A tantrum is likely to follow.

The Bribing Parent

Your child asks, 'Can I have this?' and you say, 'Yes, if you're good.' In this situation, you are essentially paying for good be-haviour and have set a standard where every time you go anywhere you've got to buy something to ensure proper be-haviour. Then if you say no, a tantrum erupts.

To avoid such problems, be decisive and take control of the situation. If you are not going to buy him a treat, tell him no before you enter the shop. Or if it's a day where he can have a little something, explain he can have one thing and that he can pick it. You be the regulator – set down what is going to happen. If you've said no and he asks again in the shop, as he most likely will, remind him of what you told him before: 'Remember, I said that today we're not getting any treats.' Stick to your word or you will have ongoing trouble. Please be okay with saying no, parents. You say yes more often.

KNOW HOW:
MAKING CAR RIDES PLEASURABLE

Part of what can make errands challenging for toddlers is the car rides. It can be boring to be strapped into a car seat for long periods of time with nothing to do. Here are my tips for making the time pass more pleasurably:

- Cars are a great place to sing songs together, recite nursery rhymes, or talk about what you are seeing out the window.

- Load songs, nursery rhymes, and stories for this age group onto an iPod, iPad, CD player or MP3 player. Play it through your car's stereo system or let him put on over-the-ear headphones to listen. (The ones that go inside the ears are often too big and can be very uncomfortable.)

- Keep a bag of books and toys in the car for entertainment and change out the items regularly.

- Carry a box with water, tissues, non-perishable snacks, a first-aid kit and lots of wipes, just in case you get stuck in terrible traffic. And don't forget a travel potty if you are working on potty training.

Avoiding Restaurant Wars

Eating out with your child can be lovely – or it can be a real nightmare. If you plan a bit in advance and follow my suggestions, you're more likely to have an enjoyable time:

- Pick a family-friendly restaurant. These have children's menus and booster seats and often offer activity sheets to draw on, even outdoor areas to run in. An added bonus is that both the staff and the other patrons are more likely to be understanding.

- Order her food first so she won't become too hungry waiting.

- Bring something for her to do at the table while she's waiting – Play-Doh or a sticker book, perhaps. Choose something that will keep her occupied and in her seat.

- Be sure to interact with your child. It's when you ignore her to focus completely on the other adults that she will tend to act up.

- Don't overstay. Children cannot sit at the table as long as adults can. Keep it short and it's more likely to be sweet. (If you are in a high-end restaurant, 8p.m. is considered adult time.)

TROUBLE-FREE PLANE, TRAIN AND CAR TRIPS

One of my favourite things about being a nanny was taking holidays with my families. I love to travel – and certainly have had more than my fair share over the years! The more you prepare in advance the easier it will be. Think about where you're going and how you're going to get there. Taking the car means you can take more luggage and stop along the way. It's also less expensive. But if it's a long trip, does it really make sense to drive ten hours each way with a three-year-old and a five-year-old in the backseat, even if you have a week in between? Planes may be quicker, but your child's ability to move around is very limited, especially if the flight is very bumpy and the seat belt sign is on for a long time.

KNOW HOW:
TRAVEL TOTE BAG

Whether you put these items in a little case that your child pulls or you carry it yourself, here are my top twelve items for two- to five-year-olds to take on trips, whether by plane, train or car:

• Finger puppets

• Etch-a-Sketch

• Music and storybooks on an iPod, iPad, MP3 player or CD player and over-the-ear headphones

• Doodle pad

• Crayons and colouring book

• Sticker books

• Pipe cleaners

• Books to read

• Activity books that have connect-the-dots, simple mazes, and colour-by-number

• Favourite blankie or stuffed animal

• Healthy snacks that don't need to be refrigerated, in plastic baggies: carrots, celery, raisins or other dried fruit, grapes, granola, little packages of crackers and cheese

• Change of clothes in case of accidents

Trains allow for more moving around, but they may not go where you want to.

Figure out in advance how to break up the time to make it more enjoyable for your child. In the car, what fun place can you stop at midway for a nice long stretch break – grab a bite to eat, go to the toilet and run around? If it's a plane ride, what can you do before or after to let her burn off energy? Can you break the trip into a few segments with stops along the way to stay for a night?

As for packing, when I worked as a nanny, I liked to pack two or three days in advance so that I didn't feel rushed. I would pin a checklist to each suitcase so that I knew not only what I put in but what needed to come back! Take as little as possible to avoid carrying a lot of luggage. You can wash clothes if necessary in your hotel room or at Grandma's house.

Pack a travel bag for each child. (See box on page 140.) Also pack a few surprises in your carry-on for when boredom with everything else sets in – a new book, a pack of cards for the four- or five-year-old. If flying, make sure you have all medications and other essentials in your carry-on in case your luggage gets lost.

I hope you are now inspired to get your little ones out on a regular basis – to enjoy the enrichment activities your community offers, as well as to venture further on trips near and far. In the next chapter, I offer my Social SOS. I'll help you get over the bumps that may occur along the way – restaurant scenes, supermarket battles and car seat challenges, to name but a few.

NINE

Social SOS

As a disciplined parent, you know the benefits of getting out and about regularly with your children and have put in place the rules I discussed in Chapter 8. But once you're out there, it doesn't necessarily go smoothly. Your child has trouble sharing in a play group. Or she's shy and hangs back, not willing to engage in an activity. Or you can't trust that she won't run off from you. Or she fights getting into the car seat and squabbles with her brother in the car. Maybe she doesn't want to leave the playground when it's time to go.

This chapter troubleshoots the common challenges parents face bringing young children into the wider world from a safety and social skills perspective. I'll deal with misbehaviour and tantrums in public in Chapters 12–15. Hopefully you will discover what you can change or tweak to make the process more enjoyable for them and for you. You may be surprised to discover that what you think of as behaviour problems are often indications of something you need to teach your child. The SOS approach helps you really explore why your child is not listening or why you are in situations that feel unsafe for him and it helps you avoid reacting out of fear.

RUNNING OFF FROM YOU

Every time you let your toddler out of the buggy, she takes off, whether she's inside a shop or outside. You are terrified of her getting lost or running out into the street where there is traffic. You don't know what you're doing wrong that she doesn't listen to you.

Step Back: Take a breath and don't react.

Observe: How long does she stay in the buggy? How often do you use it as a form of control so that she'll stay put and not move or touch anything? Have you taught her how to walk beside you safely? Have you worked on her communication skills, in particular obeying you when you say stop? Is she still very young and therefore impulsive and can't be trusted to do as you say just yet?

What do you want to achieve? Your child staying by you and stopping when you tell her to, as well as being realistic about what you can achieve right now.

Step In: The first action here is to get her walking next to you holding on to the buggy. See the Roaming technique, Parts I and

II, on pages 128 and 129. These techniques are helpful to know because most kids want to be out of the buggy unless their feet or legs are hurting from walking too much. They especially want to be out if they've been cooped up in it for too long. I would practise in the safest of places, which is an enclosed park, so that even if she does run off, she can't get into harm's way.

Also work on her following directions through games such as Red Light, Green Light or Stop/Go: When you say 'red light' or 'stop', she must freeze in place; when you say 'green light' or 'go', she can move. You can also do it with instruments: when you shake the maracas, she can dance and when you stop, she must stop. Can she do what you say when you say it? You can see how much early learning comes into play here.

However, even if your child does well at these games, you can never, ever assume that she won't surprise you and show unpredictable behaviour. Children are impulsive at these ages. Even though you practise walking side by side, you can't trust that a two- or even three-year-old will stay by you all the time. At four and five, they become more trustworthy through showing you they can listen, but even then you need to be diligent at all times, watching how they behave, so that they can have the freedom to enjoy walking while being aware of what's around them and keeping safe.

CAR SEAT BATTLES

She was fine when she was younger, but ever since she turned two, your daughter kicks and screams every time you try to put her in her car seat. In your driveway, it's bad enough, but it's downright embarrassing when you're in a car park and a driver is waiting for your spot. It's so unpleasant that you avoid taking her anywhere.

Step Back: Take a breath and don't react.

Observe: How are you handling it now? Are you avoiding the situation as much as possible by keeping her at home and dealing with it by physical force when you must take her out? What happens when she gets too big for that? Have you made clear what was expected, then given a warning and consequences for this behaviour? What's your emotional state when this is happening? Are you agitated or calm and in control?

What do you want to achieve? To have your child get into her seat calmly when you tell her to, so you can enjoy going out.

Step In: The reality is that every child must be strapped into a car seat. Car or booster seats are now a requirement in the UK for all children under 135cm and under 12 years old. Your child is not listening to you and is being defiant. This is a battle for control that has arisen as she hits the toddler years, with their drive for independence. I would use a three-step game plan to turn a situation like this around.

Step one is for you to calmly take charge, knowing that you will do what it takes to change this behaviour. The calmer and more relaxed you are, the less likely she will be to escalate.

Step two is to role-play going on a trip at home. Make it a fun game. Sit on cushions in the living room, on her bed, or in a cardboard box. Bring her car seat in and have her sit in it and help her wrap herself in. Explain to her that everyone wears a seat belt to keep them safe. Go on a pretend trip – you open your door, put on your seat belt and go somewhere fun.

Step three is to tell her what's expected the next time you get into the car: 'Remember we practised this yesterday? Get into the seat now and I'll help you strap yourself in.' If she refuses to listen:

- Crouch down about half a metre in front of her and look her in the eyes.
- Say in a low, slow voice: 'This is naughty behaviour. If you don't get into your seat right now, you will go on the Naughty Step when we get home.' (See page 218.)
- If she refuses, use your strength to put her in and follow through on the consequence when you return home. You don't use the Naughty Step now because it keeps her from getting into the car, which is what you are aiming for.
- Keep at it consistently until she learns that this is just simply something that people have to do and she does it willingly. If you don't follow through every time, she won't learn that you mean it.
- Work on her being more cooperative through fun listening games such as Simon Says and Red Light, Green Light. Also keep to a routine that minimises car time, as children easily get bored riding around.

SQUABBLES IN THE BACKSEAT

You've got three kids under the age of six and end up spending a lot of time in the car, running errands and taking them to various

activities and playdates. Inevitably they end up grabbing one an-
other's toys, yelling, poking, hitting. You try to mediate from the
front seat. The pandemonium makes for very unpleasant rides.
OMG – you realise you are going to get in an accident if you are
not careful!

Step Back: (You must do this step *mentally* because you're in
your seat buckled up.) Take a breath and don't react.

Observe: Do your children squabble every trip or only at certain times, like close to lunch or naps for the younger ones? How
long are they in the car before it begins? What do you do when it's
happening? Do you say things like 'If you don't stop, I am going
to pull this car over' but then never do? Do you follow through
with consequences for misbehaviour?

What do you want to achieve? Peaceful and safe car rides.

Step In: You are the driver and your first priority is safety.
You need to be in control at all times. From now on, when this
happens, pull over so you have a chance to take a step back, see
what's going on and put a plan into effect. I say this because so
many parents have told me that they've ended up in accidents
or near accidents from driving while trying to figure out what's
happening in the backseat.

Once you pull over, give the kids a chance to explain what
happened and then make a decision on the spot how to handle it.
You *have* to be authoritative with your expectations because this is
a life-or-death situation.

Before you get in the car the next time, establish your car
rules: (1) One game or toy at a time. (2) Seat belts and car seats. (3)

House rules in car – take turns, no hitting or yelling. If anyone violates a rule, give a warning and if it doesn't stop, explain that he'll go on the Naughty Step when he gets home or lose a privilege.

DEALING WITH JUDGMENTS OF OTHERS WHILE TRAVELLING

You're on a plane trip with your little ones. You've had to get them up early for the flight, it's been a long trip and they are whining and crying. Other people are giving you dirty looks. You think, 'This is exactly why I never want to take my kids anywhere.' You feel like a failure as a parent.

Step Back: Take a breath and don't react.

Observe: What's going on? Is there something you can do to help your kids in this moment? Are they hungry? Can you engage them in an activity? Do you need to issue a warning and then, if necessary, a consequence? Or is this a situation where there really is nothing that can be done, so you just have to stay calm and wait till it's over? What is your emotional state?

What do you want to achieve? An enjoyable trip.

Step In: If, after observing, you realise you can do something to help your kids, by all means do it. But often in these situations, what is needed is for you not to get riled by other people's judgments. It's my observation that too many of us have become intolerant of children. Everybody's overworked, overstressed and erstimulated. There's a total lack of understanding about what normal toddler behaviour. Well, this is it!

There are two types of onlookers. One is the person who will ok at you, see that you could be doing something and think, Vhy isn't he doing something about this?' That's reasonable, hich is why you make sure you've done everything you can. hen there's the type of arrogant onlooker who thinks you should able to control everything a child is doing – or make him dis-pear. Let those people go about their own business so that you n get on with yours. Focus on your child rather than others ound you. The last thing you need to worry about is other peo-e. Stay focused on what you can resolve.

OUCHES EVERYTHING IN SHOPS

You hate to take your three-year-old to shops because he won't listen. He tries to touch everything in sight and you're afraid he's going to break or take something. Plus he gets easily bored and whiny after a few stops. It's just easier to run errands without him.

Step Back: Take a breath and don't react.

Observe: Why are you avoiding taking him with you? Just so can be easier on you? Have you taught him to stay next to you? ave you taught him what he can touch and what he can't? Have u made it clear how he's supposed to behave and put warnings d consequences in place?

What do you want to achieve? His knowing how to behave in a de variety of public situations.

Step In: The supermarket, the dry cleaner's, the chemist, the shopping centre – these are places that every child should be familiar with. You should not be avoiding them because you haven't taken the time to teach your child how to behave in these settings. It's inevitable you will be going out with him at some stage, so make it easy on you both and enjoy yourselves.

Young children are curious. They see something new and want to touch it. That's natural. But you should be teaching your child at home what can and can't be touched so that he understands the concept when he goes out. Make clear what's acceptable – 'This is not a toy. It's for adults, so don't touch' – so that when he gets out into the exciting world, he is familiar with the concept.

Once you've laid that groundwork, think about where you will be going. Of course there are places that are best not to bring children. You don't want your three-year-old wandering around a shop full of china. But for the ordinary places you go to, there is no need to leave him at home. Simply set out the expectations clearly: Going to the supermarket? 'Yes, you can help Mummy pick up the fruit and vegetables.' Going to a gift shop? 'No touching.'

If there are a lot of breakables and he's with you, hold his hands and tell him not to touch anything. It should go without saying that you are responsible for anything your child breaks. Unfortunately, I walk into shops all the time and the first thing owners say to me is, 'I wish you were here every day. Parents come in and their kids break things. When I say to them, "There's a charge for that," they say, "My child didn't mean to do it." Of course your child didn't mean it. But he is your responsibility. And I'm losing stock!'

You also need to look at how much time you're spending on errands before doing something fun with your child. An hour is pretty much the limit. Otherwise, you may get not only boredom and whining but also mischievous behaviour or tantrums because he wants to play with something, anything – even if it's that very expensive knickknack that you've told him not to touch.

NOT PAYING ATTENTION IN ACTIVITY CLASS

You've signed up your three-and-a-half-year-old for a gymnastics class. While all the other three-year-olds listen to the instructor and do what she says, your son won't wait his turn in line but wanders off to watch other classes. Sometimes he does an activity and sometimes he doesn't. You wonder if he's just too young or if you should try something he might be more interested in.

Step Back: Take a breath and don't react.

Observe: Was this just the first class or has it happened more than once? Does he have this issue of not waiting in line elsewhere, such as at the playground? How does he do with following instructions at home? Has he ever been part of a group before where he had to go along with what others are doing, such as a library reading group and if so, how does he do there?

What do you want to achieve? Your child following instructions in a group so that he can get the most out of the class.

Step In: In situations like this, I would definitely not take the child out of the class. This is a learning opportunity to prepare him for a crucial skill needed for school – following instructions in a group. See page 134 in Chapter 8 for specific activities that can strengthen his ability to listen and follow instructions. You should also practise taking turns; see page 132. I would also find situations where he has to wait in a line, such as at a playground slide, so he gets more experience with that as well.

In addition to working on these skills at home, prepare him before class by reminding him what he is to do: 'We're going to class. It's going to be fun. Ms Emily is going to tell you what to do and you must listen and do just like when we played Red Light, Green Light yesterday. And you will have to wait your turn, just like you did when we went to the park and you had to wait to go up the slide. You'll have fun.'

Don't forget to heap lots of praise afterwards for the things he did right: 'Wow, Matthew, you did a great job waiting for your turn! And when Ms Emily told you to take a big jump, you did it! I am so proud of you!' Practice, preparation and praise will get a child over the hump in these circumstances.

NOT PLAYING NICELY

You hate to admit it, but your four-year-old often acts badly during the playdates you and your friends organise. She snatches toys, yells at others and sometimes even hits or throws sand. You apologise to the other mothers and explain how she's tired or cranky that day, but it's incredibly embarrassing. You

*don't understand why everyone else's child is better behaved
than yours.*

Step Back: Take a breath and don't react.

Observe: What exactly is she doing? Is she not sharing? Being
territorial about space? Is this the only place you see such naughty
behaviour, or does it occur elsewhere? What do you do when
your child behaves this way? Do you issue a warning and then
put a consequence in place? Or do you simply make excuses to
justify her behaviour? Have you taught her the basic social skills
of toddlerhood – sharing and taking turns?

*What do you want to achieve? Your child behaving nicely towards
other children and doing better socially.*

Step In: Rather than make excuses to the other parents when
your child misbehaves towards other children, you need to take
swift action using the Sideline technique (page 221) so that she
can learn how to behave towards others. Not being allowed to
be part of the action usually swiftly gets the message home. If
she snatches something from somebody else, have her give it
back.

However, that is only part of the solution. You also need to
work with your child on taking turns and sharing (see page 132).
If she doesn't practise these social skills with you, she won't know
what to do when she gets in the sandpit with someone else.

In situations like this, I would start off with one-on-one playdates and then build the numbers as she learns how to get along.
When a child is coming over, have her select the toys that are

going to be shared. Allow her to put away a special toy that she doesn't have to share.

When she goes to other children's homes, teach her about taking care of other people's toys and showing manners: 'Please, can I play with this? Thank you.' When you are driving to a playdate, remind her of how she should behave: 'We're going to play with your friends. You need to share and take turns like we practised this morning. That way you can all have fun.'

Teach her the etiquette of sharing group space, such as public swings and slides. Have her go on the swing for a little bit of time and then say, 'You've had enough time now. Let's let the little boy who's waiting have a turn.' Of course she won't want to, but you remind her that she can get back on after his turn.

SHY IN GROUPS

Whether it's in an activity class or in a play group, your three-year-old hangs back. She doesn't readily engage with others, preferring to sit on the side and observe. You want to encourage her sociability but aren't sure what to do. You worry she will have trouble making friends when she's older. Why won't she join in?

Step Back: Take a breath and don't react.

Observe: Is your child always like this or only at the beginning of a new experience? Once she's been exposed to it for a few times, how does she behave? What do you do when she's on the side? How do you help her enter in?

KNOW HOW:
HELPING TODDLERS TAKE TURNS

When there is a group of children who all want the same thing – it's Little Tikes cars and water tables these days, I've observed – parents often jump in and say, 'Take turns.' But the children are too young to figure out how to do that. Step in and help: 'We have to take turns. Okay, Jake goes first, and then Zoey and then Katie. I'll keep time and call your name and let you know when it's your turn. And meanwhile, find something else to play with while you're waiting.'

What do you want to achieve? Her being comfortable in social settings and joining in.

Step In: Some children need to watch for a while to get comfortable in a new setting or with a new activity. They need time to warm up, as it were. So let her sit there for a bit with you.

But you can't let her just sit there forever. At some point you need to coax her out to play. Bring her to where other children are and help her get involved. If it's a play group, find something she can do alongside others and do it with her for a minute or two. If it's an activity class, have her join in the activity with you by her side. Get her up and moving. Then leave, telling her you'll watch from the side. Most likely she will soon be fully engaged and having fun. But don't be surprised if you have to repeat the process in the next new situation. The more you do it, the easier it will get.

DOESN'T WANT TO DO SOMETHING

Your three-year-old son is afraid to do the circuit at the gymnastics class – along the beam, up the ladder, down the slide. He cries when he gets to the beam. Your feeling is that if he's uncomfortable, he shouldn't do it. Your husband says you should make him do it so he can overcome his fear. You ended up in an argument that resulted in a stalemate.

Step Back: Take a breath and don't react.

Observe: Exactly what is hard for him? What kind of gross motor skills are needed? What kind of coaching and support could you give to help him? What is your underlying belief about challenges – that a person should give up and not try? What do tears mean to you? Frustration? Fear? What's your automatic reaction when your child cries?

What do you want to achieve? Your child overcoming his fear and enjoying what he now feels uncomfortable about.

Step In: Parents of young children have a variety of reactions to their child crying. Of course, in this situation it means that he's afraid. But that doesn't necessarily mean he should stop what he's doing. To me, it means that he needs more help from you so he won't be so fearful. He also needs lots of reassurance and praise.

I remember looking after a little girl who cried in a very similar situation because she thought that if she screamed enough, I would give in and we would leave. Instead, I said to the rest of the families in the class, 'Excuse me, she is just getting used to this.' Then I went over next to her and gave her encouragement and coaching while supporting her: 'You got over that really well! Now go under! Yes, now go up!' Even though she was crying, I coaxed her to do it slowly. I backed this up with working on gross motor skills at home with bike riding. Over a few weeks, she got better through practice and praise. Not only did the tears go away, but she began to enjoy going off to gymnastics class.

In order to carry out such a plan, you need to truly understand that coaching and encouraging your child – to learn something even when he is afraid – is different from forcing him to do it. Forcing is unaided. It's making a child do something he's afraid of without support, encouragement or reassurance, without helping him feel safe enough to overcome the obstacle. Some-times a child does need to be nudged beyond his fear. You do it when you know he's capable of doing something. You've seen him do similar things in other circumstances, like go down the slide in your garden, but now he's in a strange place. You guide him past the hurdle so that with practise he can become more confident. You coax him past his fear, perhaps doing it with him. If I'm at one end of a tunnel and a child is at the other and doesn't want to go through, I go behind him and tickle him slightly and we go through together. Believe me, the sense of accomplishment he's going to feel once he gets past his fear will provide a base of inner strength that will help take him far!

THE BIG SIBLING TECHNIQUE

When your four-year-old starts to behave like a two-year-old because you've got a new baby, it's time for the 'Big Sibling' technique. Here's how it works:

- What are the things that you can allow him to do so he feels like the big sibling? Because you want him to think that's the best thing to be.
- Think in terms of responsibilities and privileges: 'You can go with Daddy to the museum because you're a big boy, the baby can't,' or 'You can put your shoes on by yourself because you're a big boy, the baby can't.'

TEN

Early Learning Rules

I'm passionate about parents being extremely disciplined regarding early learning because it is critical to the success of your child's development. Here's why: 85 per cent of his brain develops by the age of five, with the most dramatic growth occurring in the first three years! So what you provide now makes a *profound* difference.

I've always been a strong believer in early education. I know when I visit a home if a child isn't being stimulated enough. Often their development is delayed and I see lots of behaviour problems. Over the past decade or so, our understanding of brain science has exploded and scientists know much more about why early learning matters so much.

Obviously children aren't born programmed with a Microsoft Office suite in their heads, like a computer. The one hundred billion brain cells they are born with only connect up through the experiences they have. And not only are their brains wired during this critical period for things such as language and physical coordination, but they also develop the very *ability* to learn. The early experiences you provide actually create the base for the way your child's brain organises and functions for the rest of his life. Everything he see, hears, feels and does shapes his brain for thinking, feeling and learning from now on. That's because the brain is a 'use it or lose it' organ – only the pathways that are frequently used are kept. It actually gets rid of the pathways that aren't being used in order to strengthen the most-used ones and it is between the ages of three and five that the brain begins to sort out what to keep and what not to.

What this all means in easy-to-understand terms is that it's crucially important that you provide the right kind of stimulation now so that your toddler has the best foundation and chances for learning later. Here's just one example of how important early learning is: children who don't learn basic literacy skills before reception are three times more likely to drop out of school as

BENEFITS OF FORMAL EARLY EDUCATION

In addition to the early learning you offer your child, I would encourage you to consider enrolling your child in nursery if you can afford it, maybe one or two days a week. Children with early education show better attachment to children and adults, and score higher in thinking ability and language development.

teenagers. Without the proper brain development early on, education is more difficult. And your child can learn at home just as well as children who go to nursery.

Of course, early learning is interconnected with the other rule categories: kids learn best when they have the proper sleep and nutrition in place and when you have worked on behaviour, so that they can sit down and focus on an activity. And learning takes place not just at home but through all the experiences out in the world you provide. It goes the other way too – when you work on your child's auditory skills, for instance, you help her learn to listen and to follow instructions so that when you tell her to stop in a situation where there may be traffic ahead, she does it. Stimulation inside and outside the home, proper behaviour, eating and sleeping – they form a foundation of loving support that allows your child to blossom.

WHAT YOUR CHILD'S BRAIN NEEDS TO GROW

To help your child's brain develop optimally, you want to support her development in four key areas. When you provide enough of the right stimulation in these areas, you ensure that your child's brain is wiring up to succeed in school and in life:

- Visual, which refers to the ability to see, track with the eyes, visually sequence and recall what's been seen. This is necessary for reading and writing, as well as learning of all sorts – learning happens when a child watches others and then imitates what he's seen. Strong visual development also helps with gross and fine motor skills, visual memory and observation.

- Auditory, which is the ability to speak and listen. This is necessary for expressing thoughts and feelings and for following directions and it's a huge component in reading and writing. Research shows that the more parents talk with their children, the bigger vocabularies the children develop and the better they're likely to do in school. When you read a book over and over, you create stronger and more complex connections in your child's brain that allows him to learn language. Children who are read to frequently know more words at age two than those who have not been read to as often. Singing and listening to and playing music are also important aspects of auditory development – they've been shown to boost language, maths, listening and reasoning ability.

- Gross motor skills involve using the large muscles of the body, such as the arms, legs and trunk, in a balanced and coordinated way. This is necessary for all physical movement, as well as being able to tell your right side from the left. In addition, physical movement is crucial for brain development – it has recently been shown that exercise stimulates the area of the brain associated with learning and memory, as well as the area that helps children pay attention, plan ahead and understand consequences. Researchers also have found that physical activity improves IQ and school achievement, including scores on verbal and maths tests.

- Fine motor skills involve the ability to use the hands and fingers as well as eye-hand coordination, which are necessary for writing, typing and life skills such as tying shoes, eating with a fork and buttoning a shirt. Children also need fine motor control for eye muscles to distinguish letters and visually track words across a page – essential skills for reading and writing. Children with poor fine motor skills have been shown to have problems in school with both handwriting and writing composition, as well as lowered self-esteem.

As you can see, these four categories are very interrelated. When you read a picture book out loud to your child, for instance, you are providing both auditory and visual stimulation. And when you go to the playground and your child runs up, over and around things, you are not only providing gross motor stimulation – he is also growing parts of his brain that will help with visual, auditory and fine motor skills.

When you work with your child in these four areas, you're preparing him to be able to do well in school because you're helping him develop his ability to focus and pay attention, to concentrate, follow directions and persist through frustration. These are all necessary skills for the learning process itself.

PUTTING A PLAN IN PLACE

You don't have to become an educational expert to do what's necessary in the early learning department. There are very simple

Effects on Children of Not Enough Stimulation	Effects on Children of Getting Proper Stimulation
PHYSICAL	**PHYSICAL**
May be delayed in development	More likely to develop appropriately
May have poor body strength	More likely to be physically strong and flexible
May have poor eye-hand coordination, including poor handwriting	More likely to be coordinated
INTELLECTUAL	**INTELLECTUAL**
Lower vocabulary	Bigger vocabulary
Less ability to learn	Stronger ability to learn
May have lower IQ	Higher IQ
More likely to do poorly in school and to drop out in teen years	More likely to do well in school
Poorer judgment and decision making	Better judgment and decision making
Less likely to have a high-paying job as an adult	**EMOTIONAL**
EMOTIONAL	Through these interactions, more intimacy and bonding with parents and other children
Fewer interactions with parents and other children, so less intimacy and bonding	More likely to have healthy self-esteem
May have low self-esteem	

KNOW HOW:
SCREEN TIME

The current recommendation by the American Association of Pediatrics is no screen time whatsoever for children under two. That's because your toddler's brain needs interactions and experiences to wire properly. TV and videos are passive. Plus research has linked TV watching in young children to weight gain and aggressive behaviour. I did an experiment on my UK TV show that demonstrated that families who eat in front of the TV have children with poorer social skills and obesity. But I am a realist – even I've put a toddler in front of a TV for a short period of time, and I guess you will too. If so, please, *please* follow my guidelines:

- Limit the time to thirty minutes maximum, whether your child is watching on a TV, DVD, iPod or iPad. If it involves your toddler not doing anything but watching, no more than $\frac{1}{2}$ hour per day.

- Choose age-appropriate shows.

- Make sure you've spent at least two hours a day on mental stimulation and one hour on physical activity.

activities you can do. All it requires is the discipline to do it on a daily basis and the patience and persistence to stick to it. It's the repetition that allows your child's brain cells to wire together, which is why so much of these years is about saying and doing the same thing over and over. Yes, you may not feel like reading that book for the twentieth time that week, or playing that game again, or repeating how to put on a jacket. But that's how a child learns. Keep the big picture in mind – that you are actually shaping his brain through these activities – and it will be a bit easier.

You can use common objects you already have in your home, along with some basic books, music and toys you can borrow from the library – yes, many cities and towns have toy libraries – or buy on eBay or at charity shops. That way when he outgrows them, you can trade them in for more age-appropriate ones at little or no cost.

If your child stays home with you all day, I would encourage you to spend at least two hours a day – one hour in the morning and one hour in the afternoon – doing a variety of the activities I suggest below. Make sure that in the course of a day she is getting stimulated in all four areas, but don't always do the same activities every day. Like with food, pick things from each group and mix it up. About twenty minutes per activity is about all you can expect at the younger ages. As she gets older, you will see your child naturally expand her interest as she engages and enjoys more.

If your child goes to day care, or nursery, it's also important that you enhance what she's been doing. Find out what she's done and balance out her day with some activities that may not have

KNOW HOW:
MORNINGS ARE BEST FOR LEARNING

It's important to do learning activities in the morning because when a child has had a good night's sleep, her brain is rested and ready to learn – it's like a sponge.

been emphasised – creative play, perhaps, or craft projects or reading together. Or perhaps some running around or matching games. Give a couple of choices in a category and then let her pick. She'll feel excited about getting to choose.

Whether he stays with you at home or not, don't forget to include some of the out-of-the-house classes and activities I wrote about in Chapter 8. They count too! Now that you know how important exercise is to your child's development overall, I hope you will agree with me how important it is to get him moving. That's why I am so distressed when I see kids in buggies all day and those bicycles that have the big pole at the end where you just push them along. How are they going to build their muscles that way? How will they learn to push down and up on a pedal to move a tricycle forward? Please, please don't be a parent who allows this lack of motion. Have your child slide his feet along first on a push car, then move to a small tricycle where he pedals up and down, then to a bike.

Activities for Visual Stimulation

Ages 2–3

- Provide shape sorters and stackers from the first year on.
- Play I Spy ('I spy with my little eye . . .': something red, something round, etc.).
- Play simple matching memory games where she has to find two cards that are the same animal or colour.
- Read picture books where you ask her to find a certain object on the page, like 'find the duck', or point to a colour.
- Draw and colour with chubby crayons. Try finger-painting.

- Play catch with a beanbag, soft ball or balloon.
- Try pattern blocks, which are sets of brightly painted wooden blocks that you put together to replicate pictures of familiar objects.
- Blow bubbles for her to catch.
- Play the 'catching fish in a net' game.

Ages 4–5

- Nanny Jo's visual memory game: put four items on a tray, then take them away and ask her to remember what they were. Add more items as she gets better.
- Draw an incomplete figure and ask her to finish it.
- Offer sticker books.
- Get activity books with connect-the-dots, hidden pictures and simple mazes (or create your own).
- Show a picture and then take it away and see what she can remember of it.
- Make a pattern with coloured blocks and ask her to continue it.
- Toss balls into a laundry basket or cardboard box.
- Play card games such as Go Fish, Old Maid and Slap Jack.
- Play alphabet games.

Activities for Auditory Stimulation

Ages 2–3

- Read, read, read – see box on page 171 with my tips.
- Narrate what you're doing – 'Now we're brushing our teeth', 'Now we're going to the shop.'

- Give him simple tasks so he learns to follow directions: 'Please give me the green shirt.' Then gradually make them more complex: 'Go into your room, pick up your shoes and bring them to me, please.'

- Play games where you identify common sounds. You can buy these or make your own (see box below for the See Me, Hear Me technique).

- Play musical instruments: maracas, tambourines, bells, drums, triangles.

- Sing: 'Row, Row, Row Your Boat', 'Twinkle, Twinkle, Little Star', 'Mary Had a Little Lamb.'

- Recite nursery rhymes, especially those with movements, such as 'Itsy Bitsy Spider', 'Ring Around the Rosy', and 'The Grand Old Duke of York'.

THE SEE ME, HEAR ME TECHNIQUE

1. Record a number of sounds off the Internet: for instance, birds singing, water rushing, car noises, cow mooing, bells ringing, etc.
2. Play them for your child and see if he can identify them.
3. Another option is to download pictures and see if your child can make sounds to match.

Ages 4–5

- Download audio stories to an iPod or MP3 player, or copy them to a cassette tape or CD. After listening, ask questions about what your child heard.

- Read longer books with more words.
- Make up your own adventure stories together: 'So the pirate Will jumped from the boat and said . . .'
- Play Silly Directions. You say something like, 'Go into the kitchen, get a plastic container from the bottom drawer and wear it on your head back here' – the sillier the better. Then your child gives you a challenge.
- Copy sound patterns. Have your child close his eyes while you clap your hands, play a drum or bounce a ball. Then have him repeat the pattern.
- Find the sound. Hide a ticking timer or a music box in a room and have him find it. Place it at different levels – low shelf, up high – so he practises locating sounds all around.

Activities for Gross Motor Stimulation

Ages 2–3
- Big blocks
- Push and pull toys
- Ride-on toys that he pushes with his feet, later switching to a tricycle that must be pedalled
- Empty laundry basket to climb in and over and push and pull around
- Dancing
- Big balls to roll, throw and catch
- Obstacle course of cushions and pillows
- Pretend animals: 'Hop like a bunny, leap like a tiger . . .'
- Jump in and out of a hula hoop

KNOW HOW:
HOW TO READ TO YOUR CHILD

Ages 2–3

- Let your child pick the book he wants.

- Read the same stories over and over so he can begin to make the connection between the words and the pictures.

- Dramatise with your voice the action in the story and give different voices to the characters.

- Ask him to name what's going on in the picture: 'Where is the cow?'

- Let him fill in missing words: 'Said the ___ in the Hat.'

Ages 4–5

- Help him connect words to sounds by moving your finger under the words as you read.

- Have him sound out simple words with you.

- Ask him what he thinks is going to happen or who he likes best in the story.

- Ask questions about the book – 'Where did the fox run to?' 'Why do you think he was scared?'

- After you've finished reading the book, draw a picture about something in the story.

Ages 4–5

- Balls of various sizes to toss, kick and catch
- Wheelbarrow walking, crab walking
- Simon Says; Red Light, Green Light
- Floor puzzles
- Skipping rope, hopscotch, tag, hide-and-seek
- Small-size plastic bat and ball
- Tug-of-war

Fine Motor Skills

Ages 2–3

- Play-Doh
- Lego
- Nesting and stacking blocks
- Simple puzzles with knobs for pincer control
- Pavement chalk
- Leftover plastic containers that can be used to pour or scoop sand or water
- Mr Potato Head
- Large beads to thread
- Collages from found objects – leaves, pebbles, popcorn, feathers, acorns

Ages 4–5

- Cutting with blunt plastic scissors
- Moulding, rolling and cutting Play-Doh with cutters and scissors

- Cutting fringe on the bottom of a piece of paper and making simple snowflakes by folding and cutting paper
- Put an object in a bag and see if he can guess what it is by touch, then have him do it for you
- Stencils to trace
- Plastic bowling set
- Keep a balloon in the air
- Beading kits
- Flower rubbings
- Building sets of gears, logs or cubes that snap together; snap circuits that light up when put together
- Train and car sets
- More complex puzzles

EXPANDING ATTENTION SPAN

Attention, focus, concentration and problem solving go hand in hand. If you have a longer attention span, it allows you to focus more on the activity you are engaged in. And if you're focused, then you can concentrate. And if you concentrate, then you can problem-solve. And if you problem-solve, you end up accomplishing the task.

Attention ⟹ Focus ⟹ Concentration ⟹ Problem Solving

I feel strongly that we need to help toddlers work on concentration and expanding their attention – to sit down for increasing periods of time, look at something thoroughly and work through

BEST BOARD GAMES FOR YOUNG CHILDREN

Ages 3+
Generally board games are not appropriate for children under three, as they have small parts that can be swallowed. These are good choices for children three and older:

Snakes and Ladders

Hi Ho Cherry O

Memory

Candyland

Cariboo

Elefun

Ages 4+

Hungry, Hungry Hippos

Sorry

Jenga

Connect 4

it carefully. If you don't do this in these crucial years, the brain circuits don't grow and then you see all kinds of problems with attention later.

One of my biggest fears is that school-age children end up getting labelled as having ADHD (see box on page 177) and are given medication when parents could have put in the early training that may have nipped these problems in the bud or at least made them less severe. I wonder how many children diagnosed with ADHD may not have a neurological condition but rather be suffering from a lack of time being put in on education in the early years to help develop those brain circuits and increase the ability to focus and concentrate.

To help your child strengthen focus and attention, make sure you have times in the day when he sits down to do an activity. Whether it's a fifteen-minute animated video, a puzzle or arts and crafts, make sure he physically sits down to do it. Teach him that there are places where we do certain things. This will help not only when he goes to school but also with sitting at the table for meals. In Chapter 11, I give other ideas for stretching attention span. When you spend time on this, you give your child the very best start no matter what his inborn tendencies are. If you end up seeing a doctor about attention issues, he or she will most likely give you similar things to do.

CREATIVE PLAY

It's important that your child has daily imaginative play as well – time with paints, glitter and glue; with bubbles, water and Tupperware containers at the sink; with crayons, fabric and boxes. I've found that most parents don't mind imagination – as long as things are kept tidy. That's a problem. Young children need to be messy. It's part of learning.

Of course, these activities have to be supervised. Especially with young toddlers who still put things in their mouths, you have to be careful around arts and crafts supplies. And of course never let him out of your sight for even a second when water is involved.

Perhaps you settle him at the kitchen table with crayons, glitter, paper and glue. That way you can make dinner and still interact and supervise.

Imaginative play also includes all the mini-world toys and activities – train and farm sets, pretend kitchen and shopping, dress-up clothes, action figures, finger puppets and dolls, face paint and non-toxic make-up. This is where kids' imaginations can go wild: the quilt becomes a cape, the box a race car, the scarf fairy wings.

With imaginative play, you have to expect a certain volume of noise as well as mess. Kids scream when they're happy. But some parents try to stifle any noise. When you do that, you're basically saying, 'Don't be happy.' Get in there and enjoy it with her. Play dress-up together. Ask her about what she's drawn. You may hear the most amazing story: 'Well, that's the duck. And then it's in the train there . . .' You look at the scotble and think, 'Wow, so *that's* what's going on in my child's mind!'

Give him time to play on his own as well. That's when he gets the space to be imaginative and make up stories. I don't think it's right for you to play with him 24/7. Yes, be involved, but sit back sometimes. You'll learn even more about what he needs when you sit back and watch.

THE IMPORTANCE OF TEACHING LIFE SKILLS

Part of early learning is also teaching your child life skills: things such as dressing and undressing, brushing hair and teeth, using utensils, picking up after himself. This is important because of

SIGNS OF ADHD

ADHD is attention deficit hyperactivity disorder (it's also called ADD, or attention deficit disorder). It can show up in a child in one of three ways: inattentive, but not hyperactive or impulsive; hyperactive and impulsive, but not inattentive; inattentive, hyperactive and impulsive. Here are the signs of each, plus ideas to deal with them.

Signs of Inattentiveness

- Has trouble staying focused; is easily distracted. *Create a peaceful environment.*

- Appears not to listen when spoken to. *Get down to his level and look him in the eyes before speaking.*

- Has difficulty remembering things and following instructions. *Play memory games.*

- Gets bored with a task before it's completed. *Take it in steps daily.*

- Frequently loses or misplaces things.

Signs of Hyperactivity

- Constantly moving, fidgeting and/or squirming.

- Trouble sitting still. *Time him getting better (see page 188).*

- May be short-tempered. *Massage, deep breathing.*

Signs of Impulsivity

- Can't wait for turn in line or in games. *Practise at home.*

- Frequent angry outbursts or temper tantrums.

- Often interrupts.

Since these characteristics are typical of children ages two to five, it can be hard to tell at these ages if there is a problem. If you are concerned, see your doctor. And remember – whether there is a problem or not, the early learning basics will help!

the natural drive for independence that occurs at the toddler stage. They *want* to do things for themselves and can experience great frustration and even tantrums when they can't. It's your job to help them become more independent.

When you work on life skills, you're also helping your child with auditory, visual and gross and fine motor skills development and when you work on auditory, visual and motor skills in other learning activities, you're helping him build the capacity to master life skills. For instance, threading beads on a string prepares a child to eventually have the eye-hand coordination to tie his shoes.

I've always been a big believer in teaching life skills when I see a child is ready. Recently I learned just why it matters so much. Researchers have discovered that in order to develop the higher-functioning area of the brain, the prefrontal cortex, children *must* be able to do things for themselves and experience the sense of accomplishment that comes from that independence.

To teach life skills, you must do four things:

KNOW HOW: TURNING BITS AND BOBS INTO TODDLER TREASURES

- Boxes of all sizes – big ones for making playhouses or castles; medium ones for building spaceships, cars or trucks to sit in; little ones to decorate and store treasures in.

- Leftover aluminium foil and wrapping paper – great for covering boxes.

- Big buttons that can't be swallowed, elbow macaroni and Cheerios for making necklaces.

- Scraps of felt and other fabric to glue together and make hand puppets.

- Dried beans and plastic bottles with screw-on lids to make maracas. Be sure to tape the lid shut so your child can't open it and swallow the beans; supervise carefully while constructing.

- Brown paper bags to make masks – animals, storybook characters, etc. You cut and they colour. Then you poke a small hole on either side and tie around the back of their heads with kitchen string.

- Cucumbers, potatoes or kitchen sponges that you can cut into shapes for them to make block print paintings using finger paint or nontoxic poster paint.

- Costume jewellery, Mummy's and Daddy's old clothes, hats, scarves and shoes for dress-up.

- Socks to make puppets.

1. Give her the time to do it.
2. Encourage her to stick to it and not give up when she gets frustrated or disengaged.
3. Offer coaching and support without taking over.
4. Give her the chance to do it over and over.

Here are my tips for making this process go smoothly:

- Pick a specific time when you are not rushed. Feeling pressured doesn't help you or her.
- Have her do it with you – put your hand on hers and guide her to brush her teeth or hair or manipulate a fork or pour milk into a bowl.
- Once she gets the hang of it, let her try it herself. You can always go back over her teeth or sunscreen application after. And remember – spills and messes come with learning. Just mop up without making a big deal out of it.
- Coach from the sidelines if necessary, in simple language. If you see she's holding the fork sideways, say, 'Turn it like this', and demonstrate.
- Offer encouragement and praise; 'You can do it!' 'Good for you, you got it!' If she can't quite get it, tell her that you know she will soon be able to do it.
- Don't jump in too soon to rescue. Frustration is part of the process. It builds determination and persistence, two very important capacities for success in every part of life. Remind her she can do it. Get even more specific in your coaching: 'Put your finger right here and try again.' Let her try to work it out.

- If she gets really frustrated, help her calm down and try again. If she still can't do it, see if you can break it down into smaller parts. Can you put the button halfway through and then she pushes it the rest of the way? Continue to practise with her over the next few days or weeks till she has it down. The feeling of accomplishment she will get will be priceless! She'll want to do it again because of the high that comes with achievement.

- Once she's mastered one skill, move on to the next. If she can easily get clothes off, for instance, teach her how to put them on. If she can put them on, start on zips and buttons.

Now you understand the basics of what you should be teaching your child and how. In Chapter 11, I will help you handle the problems that can arise in this area – what to do to help your child sit down and get involved in an activity, how to expand his attention and how to handle common issues that arise around teaching life skills.

ELEVEN

Early Learning SOS

I hope that after reading why early learning is so important, you are all fired up about providing your child with the right amount and kinds of stimulation. You understand the relationship between behaviour problems and a lack of work on early learning basics such as listening, following directions and attention span. You also know how important it is to teach your child age-appropriate life skills. You've got a plan and are ready to engage.

But what if your child won't cooperate? She won't sit still. You give her a toy and she's on to the next thing in two seconds. She won't listen when you try to read her a book. She makes a mess of the art supplies. She can't brush her teeth properly. You have a sense that this should be fun, but you find yourself frustrated.

The SOS of early learning is all about recognising how you can get the most out of your child's ability to learn and what you need to do to support that process better. At these ages, a child learns primarily through play and exploration, not structured lessons. The tips and techniques in this chapter will help ensure not only that you are giving your child the proper start but also that the process is enjoyable for the two of you. The Step Back will help you to stay calm, while Observation will give you clues about what to put in place in order to increase her learning and enjoyment. Then you Step In with a plan that leads to success.

PLAYING ALONE

Your child, who's two, can't seem to play on his own for even a few minutes. He follows you around from room to room and wants you to play everything with him. You don't want to turn into his playmate, but that's exactly what's happening.

Step Back: Take a breath and don't react.

Observe: Have you taught him how to play on his own? When you give him something to play with, does he know what to do with it? For instance, if he has a farm animal set, have you gone through the noises that the animals make and what they do so that he can then do it on his own? Is he going through a stage where he's quite clingy anyway so he wants you when he's playing because he wants you wherever you go?

What do you want to achieve? His ability to play by himself.

Step In: Playing alone is an important skill that forms part of the basis of independence, creativity and imagination. The inability to play alone seems to be more common in boys, who

NAUGHTY BEHAVIOUR OR SIGNS OF UNDERSTIMULATION?

Many so-called behaviour problems are really due to a lack of physical, mental and social stimulation. You may see trouble falling asleep because a child has not burned up enough energy during the day. Or naughty behaviour during the day because he is bored. I'm not saying that naughty behaviour shouldn't be corrected. But discipline alone won't solve the problem if you don't also provide enough activity that he can engage in.

Take a hard look at how your child spends his day. Is it a good routine that provides sixty minutes of physical activity? Is he having one to two hours of learning supervised by you, the babysitter, or the day care or nursery teacher? Does he get out to play with others regularly? Does he do regular creative and imaginative play? Is he read to every day? Tell yourself the truth and think about what you should be adding in. Your reward will be better behaviour on your child's part, behaviour you will all be proud of.

are generally emotionally more needy and less self-sufficient than girls. However, all toddlers go through phases of separation anxiety, which can interfere with this process.

That's why I developed my Play and Stay, Play Away technique. (See next page.) It teaches a child to play alone while simultaneously taking the reality of separation anxiety into account. Because you come and go around the house, it reassures your child that you're always there, which gives him confidence to play on his own. Before you leave him, make sure he knows what to do with the activity you've chosen. Over time, he'll get comfortable with you being away, knowing you are still around and he will enjoy playing alone, whether that's with his farm animals, trucks or rocking horse.

THE PLAY AND STAY, PLAY AWAY TECHNIQUE

1. Make sure your house is child-safety proofed.
2. Play with her for a bit and then say, 'Mummy's going to go to the kitchen, I'll be back in a minute.' You want her to be engaged in something she can do by herself before you go: blocks, easy puzzles, etc.
3. Walk out of the room confidently, talking to her from the other room so she can hear your voice. Stay away for one minute, then come back. You don't want to leave your child unattended for a long period of time. This is just to show her that you may go into another room, but you always come back.
4. Do this at various times and in various places so she'll learn through repetition that you always come back.

WANTS TO BE ON YOU ALL THE TIME

Your eighteen-month-old is glued to your hip. You don't know how to get her off you so that she can learn to play by herself.

Step Back: Take a breath and don't react.

Observe: What do you do when she lifts her arms and cries to be picked up?

What do you want to achieve? Her being able to be comfortable playing near you without feeling insecure.

Step In: My Off the Hip technique (see below) is designed to get your toddler off you and down on the ground so that she can learn to play on her own and move on in her development. Remember there is a difference between meeting a child's need for a warm cuddle and teaching her to be okay with not being attached to you always. This helps to create healthy boundaries, stability and safety.

THE OFF THE HIP TECHNIQUE

1. When she cries to be picked up, come down to her level and keep her at arm's length.
2. Tell her calmly and confidently you're not going to pick her up and what you're going to be doing, for instance, 'I'm making the dinner now. It's okay.'
3. If she follows you crying for you (and she will), crouch back down at arm's length again and say, 'I'm busy doing this right now. You can go and play with your toys. Or you can watch me. Then we can get back to having some fun in a moment.'
4. Eventually she will see it's okay to play around you, knowing that you are busy doing other things too.

GETS EASILY FRUSTRATED

You've been doing activities with your two-and-a-half-year-old and she seems to get very easily frustrated. If, for instance, she tries to put a puzzle piece in and doesn't get it right the first time, she just gives up. Sometimes she even throws the piece in anger. How do you encourage her to stick with it and work it out?

Step Back: Take a breath and don't react.

Observe: Is this an activity that is appropriate for her level of development? In other words, is she capable of doing it? If so, what do you do when she starts to get frustrated? Are you encouraging? Do you help her figure it out? Do you teach her to calm down and keep trying? Do you praise her when she does it right? What do you do if she throws something?

What do you want to achieve? Greater persistence, patience and problem-solving skills, no throwing things or having tantrums.

Step In: First, make sure that the activities you are giving her to do are at her developmental level. You might even want to go back to something she was able to do before for a bit. Then go on to something more challenging. If she's having trouble with a puzzle, for example, mentally she may know where a piece goes but lacks the fine motor skills to put it in place. Your job is to help her learn how to work it out for herself. If she starts to get frustrated, step in with verbal help. Say, 'You can do it. Just take your hand and move the piece around.' Put your hand over hers and fit the piece in with her if she's really having trouble figuring it out. Then heap on the praise: 'You did it!

I'm proud of you!' and encourage her to go on to the next piece straightaway.

If your daughter throws something, explain that throwing is naughty behaviour. If she does it again, use the Naughty Step (see page 218). With your gentle but decisive coaching and encouragement, she will learn how to persist to meet with success.

SHORT ATTENTION SPAN

Your four-year-old seems to have a shorter attention span than your friend's child. He flits from game to game in his room, never seeming to complete anything. His room looks like a bomb went off in it, with toys that he's played with only for a few moments strewn everywhere. You don't know how to help him.

Step Back: Take a breath and don't react.

Observe: Where are you when he's doing this? Are you interacting with him or just sending him off to play? What do you do to get him back into an activity? Do you just let him move on to the next toy? Is he distracted by all the other things in his room, so his focus is not on that particular activity? Have you taught him to put what he's been playing with away before moving on to the next thing?

What do you want to achieve? Longer attention span so he will be able to focus, concentrate and enjoy what he has accomplished.

Step In: In order to increase your child's attention span, you need to get more involved. Do an activity with him and time how long he spends on it. Then encourage him to stick to it one minute more. For instance, if he's colouring for five minutes and wants to get up, encourage him to stay and colour for one more minute: 'What colour do you think this part should be?' Use a timer so you can measure progress. The next day, add another minute more. Leave it at that time frame for a few days, then add three minutes. Keep at it so that he eventually can focus for twenty minutes on one thing. That is entirely doable at the ages of two through five.

But you have to sell him on staying with it. Coax him: 'Look, you're almost done. What other colour might go there? What about some blue? This is fun! When we're done, we get to look at the whole picture.' Make sure you're engaged in the activity too. Your active involvement will encourage him to focus.

Don't just put a toy in front of him and tell him to play with it. Kids this age need help understanding how to engage with a toy: 'Look, you put this thing here and then the ball goes round and round.' Be enthusiastic: 'You're going to love this. It's really fun. See how you push this here and pull that there?'

To prevent him from being distracted by other toys, his room needs to be somewhat tidy. Teach him to put the toy or game he's been playing with away before taking something else out.

NOT TALKING

Your twenty-month-old is not talking very much, mostly bab-bling. Your doctor says his hearing is fine, so you shouldn't be concerned – kids develop at their own pace. But you worry any-way. You want to make sure you are doing everything you can to support his language development.

Step Back: Take a breath and don't react.

Observe: What are you doing now to support his language development? Are you narrating everything you are doing? Are you asking him questions but not answering them for him? When you speak, do you face him so he can see you? Are you reading every day to him?

What do you want to achieve? Supporting his speech development.

Step In: The game plan to support language development has several steps: First, you need to talk, talk, talk to your child about what you are doing. It may feel strange to be offering a constant running commentary on your activities, but it really helps: 'Now we're washing our hands. Daddy is putting on his coat. Now we're getting into the car.'

Second, when they initially learn language, children can understand more than they say. So play the 'Where are your toes? Where's your ear?' game often. When you read books or do puzzles, have him point out where the cat, bird and sheep are. Sounds are easier than words, so ask, 'What noise does the cat make? What noise does the cow make?' Eventually he will make the sound, then connect the name of the animal to it.

Make sure you are asking him questions but not answering them for him. Give him time to answer, because at some point he will! A friend of mine was doing this one day with her two-year-old. She asked, 'Do you want more juice?' and her daughter replied, 'More.' It was her very first word.

When you are talking to your child, make sure he can see your face. I've always been a strong believer in face-to-face communication. Recently my findings were backed up by new research showing that children learn to talk not only from hearing language but also from reading our faces, both our mouths and our eyes. So make sure he can see you.

DOESN'T LISTEN

Your two-and-a-half-year-old doesn't seem to listen to you. You ask her to do something, such as get dressed, but she ignores you. You're not sure if she's being defiant.

Step Back: Take a breath and don't react.

Observe: Exactly when doesn't she listen? Does she have trouble when it's something fun to do or only when it's a task she might not like? Are you getting down to her level and talking face-to-face when you ask her to do something or are you yelling from another room? Are you getting any visual confirmation that she understands what you're saying? Or that she understands but doesn't want to do it, like a frown or pout? Are you asking your child to do things that are too complex for a toddler this age to do on her own, such as 'Go get dressed' or 'Go brush your teeth'? Are you helping, encouraging and coaching when you ask her to do something like getting dressed? Or is she on her own, getting frustrated and losing sight of what to do?

What do you want to achieve? Her doing as you say.

Step In: If you've concluded that it's a matter of her not understanding, then you know you need to teach her to follow directions. Play one of her musical instruments and have her follow the sound around the house. Play Simon Says and Red Light, Green Light.

Give her simple directions during the day. Start with something you are asking her to do that she does right there in the room with you. Look her in the face and say: 'Please, can you pick up that truck and hand it to me?' Break bigger tasks into smaller pieces. Don't tell her to tidy her room. That's too hard. Say instead, 'Can you pick up the teddy bear and put it on the shelf, please?' Once she does that, then ask her to put away the next thing. As she gets better, you can increase the complexity so that by the time she's four you can say: 'Please pick up your dress off the floor, put it in your room and then come into the living room,' and she can do it on her own.

Make sure you are very specific and simple in your language when teaching her a life skill. Do it next to her. Take out your toothbrush and toothpaste, say, 'Put the toothpaste on the brush like this,' and show her what to do. Then have her do it. Shadow by putting your hand on hers so she can get the feel of the movement.

WON'T SIT WITH YOU TO READ

You understand the importance of reading and you read – or at least try to read – to your three-year-old every night. But he won't stay on your lap for the whole story. He wanders around and you end up spending the whole time threatening that if he doesn't come back he will have to go straight to bed without a story.

Step Back: Take a breath and don't react.

Observe: While he's moving around, is he still listening to you? Does he come back to you and look at a picture? Or does he get fully engaged with something else, totally ignoring the story? When he wanders off, do you try to engage him in the story – 'Wait, look at what the bunny is doing now!' Or do you become very stern and order him back?

What do you want to achieve? A positive reading experience that supports your child's literacy development and makes for a fun time before bed.

Step In: Kids this young often move around a bit while listening to a story, but you can tell they are still engaged because they come back, look at a picture, maybe answer a question you ask. That's fine. As their attention spans grow, they will be able to sit longer.

Tell him at bath time that after he puts on pajamas, you're going to read him a story and he gets to pick the book. Read in the living room to reduce distractions or if it's in his room, put other toys out of sight. Let him turn the pages. Put on a performance while reading – ham it up, use different voices. This will help keep him more interested. If he begins to wander away, ask questions to bring him back to the story: 'What is the princess going to do next?' If he's misbehaving a lot and not listening at all, I would use the Loss of Privilege technique for the next day (page 225), then go back to the book.

MAKING A MESS

You want to fuel your children's imagination and creativity. And the two of them, ages two and four, love to finger-paint, use an easel, play with glitter and glue. But they make such a mess everywhere that you're reluctant to get out the paint box. When you try to do a structured art project, they don't listen to you. You want them to learn to be neater and follow your instructions better before you do more art projects.

Step Back: Take a breath and don't react.

Observe: Is not wanting a mess a good reason not to let them have the chance to be creative on a regular basis? Do you allow time for unstructured creative play as well as specific art projects? Are they maybe not listening because they want to have a chance to experiment with the materials?

What do you want to achieve? A chance for your children to play creatively.

Step In: I often see this problem with mothers who have become so stressed because they're not in control of their lives that they seek to tightly control their children. They don't want to clear up the mess. They're worried that it's going to take too much of their time. They don't understand how to let go and enjoy the playful experiments that are happening. The toddler years are, by definition, messy. Kids have grass and dirt stains on their clothes, paint on their hands . . . Let go of the stress of mess and let your children have the freedom to be creative.

Choose a place where you won't have to overly restrict them. I've seen parents set things up and then immediately start with: 'Be careful! Don't put that there! Pick that up!' Do it in a room that can be mopped. Have them put on old clothes or one of Daddy's old shirts. Put newspaper down on the floor. Put a plastic tablecloth on the table. Let the organised chaos happen and then clear it up after.

I don't have a problem with age-appropriate structured art projects. Just make sure your children also have time to experiment with the materials instead of always having to create a specific project. And let go of what it is 'supposed' to look like so you can enjoy what they end up making. It doesn't have to be picture-perfect – because in their eyes, it is!

I DON'T KNOW HOW TO PLAY WITH MY KIDS

You work all day and at the weekend your kids are always saying to you, 'Daddy, let's play!' You want to play with them, to connect and have fun. But you don't know what to do and soon they lose interest and run off. You feel like you're letting them down.

Step Back: Take a breath and don't react.

Observe: How are you approaching this situation? Like it's a job? A task to cross off your list? Do you feel as though your children are watching and judging you like they're your boss? Do you feel like there's some kind of magic formula that you don't have?

What do you want to achieve? To tap into your own creativity and imagination so you can play with your kids and in return they will have fun playing with you.

Step In: Play takes a different mind-set than work. Especially with young children, there is no one evaluating you. You aren't going to be graded or receive a promotion or demotion. All your children want is for you to do things with them. They really don't care what it is or how you do at it. All you need is the willingness to let your hair down and be silly, silly and more silly.

One place to start is to act out a story they've recently read. If it's about a bear who gets lost in the woods and gets rescued by two mice, go into the garden. One of you be the bear, the other two the mice. Act out the story and then take it from there. What do the mice do next? Where does the bear go? Starting with someone else's story is a good way to ignite your own creativity.

Don't be afraid to look silly, because kids this age love silly. I once helped a single dad who didn't know how to play with his toddler daughter. I encouraged him to play dress-up with her – and you should have seen her face when she saw her father in a boa and hat. They had so much fun that he got over the embarrassment and now can host a teddy bear tea party in full costume with the best of them! It's about just letting loose!

TWELVE

Good Behaviour Rules

Just as you must provide food, sleep, exploration outside the house and mental and physical stimulation for your child, you also must teach her proper behaviour – what is acceptable and unacceptable in how we treat other human beings, what is safe and unsafe to do and the difference between right and wrong.

As a parent who embraces conscious parenting, which I discussed in Chapter 1, you know it's part of your job as a parent to shape your child's behaviour. You know it's not your neighbour's job. Or the school's. Or your best friend's. It's yours.

You also now know that it becomes more challenging to change a child's behaviour the older she gets because her brain has deeply grooved pathways from how she's behaved in the first five years. It's easier to shape her behaviour in the first few years because her wiring is just getting set up. That's why it's so important to do it now.

Good behaviour is strongly tied to my four other rules. If you don't have sleeping, eating, early learning and socialisation in hand, you'll see all kinds of behaviour issues. And when you establish the basics of good behaviour, the other four categories of my toddler rules will go more smoothly. Being able to share space, toys and company with another toddler; to enjoy sitting down and eating a meal with you; to be able to follow instructions to get the most out of an activity like a music class – these are all influenced by good behaviour.

Ultimately the result of shaping positive behaviour well in the toddler years is a child who is happy to learn, to socialise, to listen to you – a child who enjoys life every day. Everything's available to her to make the most of, because behaviour is not an issue. And you enjoy parenthood so much more because every day is not a battle.

EIGHT STEPS TO POSITIVE BEHAVIOUR

How do children learn to behave? As he becomes mobile, a child starts to explore his world and discover what is acceptable and not acceptable to do. He does something, experiences your pleasure or displeasure and learns for the future from your response. That means you need a combination of teaching positive behaviour and using effective discipline techniques to curb naughty behaviour when necessary. In Chapter 13, I'll discuss discipline techniques to use when your child misbehaves. This chapter focuses on what you need to put in place so that your child learns positive behaviour.

Effects on Children of Not Learning Proper Behaviour	Effects on Children of Learning Proper Behaviour
EMOTIONAL	**EMOTIONAL**
Impulsivity	Good impulse control
Immaturity	Empathy
Lack of empathy	Sense of safety
Sense of being out of control	**SOCIAL**
Irrationality, poor reasoning	Able to get along well with others
SOCIAL	Fit well in groups
Unable to get along well with others	**INTELLECTUAL**
Disruptive in groups – can't play well with others	Able to listen and conform, ask questions, problem-solve
Negative behaviour to get attention	Academic performance to potential
INTELLECTUAL	
Trouble learning because he won't listen or conform	
Poor academic performance – won't follow through, work things out	

Parents teach positive behaviour through love, through praise, through showing a child how to behave, through mirroring the behaviour you want to see. This allows your child's spirit to remain intact and her personality to grow. To make it easy for you, I've broken it down into eight steps. And I've even distilled those down into three simple actions (see box). If you put these eight steps in place, you will go a long way towards giving your child the best start in becoming a loving, caring, responsible, respectful human being.

THREE SIMPLE STEPS TO POSITIVE BEHAVIOUR

1. Tell him what to do.

2. Show him how to do it.

3. Praise and reward when you see him do it right.

1. Decide What Matters to You

The first thing you must do is to recognise the kind of behaviour that you want to see from your child. For instance: *I want my child to be someone who is able to share with other children and to be able to enjoy the experience of playing with friends. I want my child to be kind to others in words and actions. I want her to understand that we respect our belongings and that there are certain rules in our home. I want her to be a respectful, decent human being who can get along well with others in her adult life.*

What is important to you and your partner as you're raising your child? Because that's what you're going to be instilling. Is it important for him to learn to pick up after himself and not jump on the furniture or does that not matter so much to you? Do you care if he scotbles on the walls or not? Understand that whatever behaviour you want to see in your child, he is going to take to the outside world as well. He'll think that *every* adult thinks the same as you.

What I'm really asking you to think about is what messages you will be giving your children. Some will be about their own behaviour. Some will be about the respect for belongings and their home. Others will be about how they treat other people.

As you think about it, you'll probably take some things from your own upbringing and others you learned as an adult. Still others will become clearer to you as you interact with your child and start to realise what's not okay and what is. Be as clear as possible up front, because if you change your mind every week about what's important to you, that sends your child mixed messages and disables her from reaching your realistic expectations.

2. Set Boundaries

Now take what matters to you and create house rules (see box on page 203). House rules are boundaries, like a white picket fence that keeps a child safe while allowing her to roam. Boundaries create freedom for your child to be free-spirited and grow in a way that is respectful to your family values and conducive to getting along with others.

Let's get something straight: regardless of whether you want to create boundaries or whether she protests against them, a child needs them. She needs them in order to be safe and to behave in a way that is respectful to herself and others. Your child doesn't want a cool bath when her temperature is 40°C. But she needs that bath to bring down her fever, so you give it to her even though you know she's going to cry and be upset. The same is true for boundaries. That's why parenting takes so much discipline – you do it because it's right, even if it doesn't feel good in the moment. Being a parent means sometimes doing things you don't want to do but need to do. Remember, being a good parent means having the discipline to do what you must do!

Boundaries don't feel good because as soon as you put them in place, your child is going to test them. It's only by testing that she learns what the parameters are and whether you really mean what you say. Remember, boundaries have to be broken to be established. Some toddlers learn very quickly that when they push a boundary, there's a consequence that they don't like, so they don't push again. Others who are more strong-willed will keep testing to see whether it's still the same the next day and the day after.

THE TALKING BOX TECHNIQUE

Here's a way to make sure you are talking with your partner about what behaviour you want:

- Create a box and fill it with blank cards.

- Both you and your partner write what you would like to discuss, one item per card.

- Spend half an hour each night going through the box. Cap the time, so you don't go around in circles.

- Don't move on to the next card until the previous one is resolved.

- By focusing on the question in the box and not each other, it's easier to let go of the fear of how the other person will react.

- The important thing is to listen to how the other person feels, talk about a resolution and then move on.

3. Communicate Boundaries and Expectations

Once you know what your house rules and boundaries are, you need to communicate them. Because children are just learning

SAMPLE 'HOUSE RULES'

Write down your house rules even though your children can't yet read, because it helps you put them in very simple language and to remember them as well! Aim for as few as possible that cover the bases. Here's an example:

- No hitting, play nice and do as you're told.

- Please listen and be kind with your words.

- Look after your toys and be kind to our pets.

and their language ability is very limited, you have to be very precise and consistent about what they can and cannot do. Keep it very black and white at this age – they can either touch something or they can't. They can either go near something or they can't. Parents are often not clear enough about what is acceptable or not. Sometimes they let her touch something and other times not. This is very confusing to a young child. A rule is a rule as far as a young child is concerned. Learning to be decisive will help your parenting.

Parents also make the mistake of going into long, detailed explanations of the rules that go over their child's head: 'Daddy doesn't want you to throw that because it could put someone's eye out and then they would be blind.' Be as straightforward as possible: 'No throwing. Someone could get hurt.' (See box on next page.)

Give examples of the behaviour you want to see so she can begin to understand what you mean: 'See how you are patting the cat right now? That's nice. That's what I want to see.'

In addition to explaining house rules, when you are about to go into a particular situation, make clear to your child what you expect from him. If you are clear in your expectations, your child wants to meet them, as he is born wanting to please. For instance, 'We're going to a restaurant with our friends. I want you to sit in your seat nicely and not get down without asking me.' Or 'Jason is coming over to play and I want you to share your toys with him.' Parents often forget to do this and then they are upset when their child misbehaves. If you haven't told him what to do, how can you expect him to do it this time and remember for next time?

While it's always good to set expectations in advance, if you're going to the supermarket with a child who's quite easygoing, you

KNOW HOW: COMMUNICATE SO YOUR CHILD WILL LISTEN

When you are stating your boundaries and expectations, communicate in such a way that your child receives the message. Otherwise you end up repeating yourself or seeing misbehaviour because he wasn't paying attention to you. Here are my tips:

- Get close to him, no more than three feet away.

- Get down to his level so you are face-to-face.

- Make eye contact.

- Use an authoritative tone of voice that conveys both conviction and respect.

- Express yourself in simple, straightforward language: 'I want you to put your book away on this shelf now.'

have the flexibility to handle it on the spot. If he says, 'Can I have this sweet?' and you say, 'No, we're not buying anything that's not on the list,' he's more likely to be accepting of your answer and less likely to have a tantrum. On the other hand, if you're dealing with a strong-willed child, make sure to do it in advance: 'We're going to the store. We're not getting anything that's not on the list.' I like to set expectations in either situation, but with a more intense child, you must make it extremely clear what is going to happen and be very certain to follow through if he misbehaves.

Consistency in boundaries and limits is so important! Please work hard to get on the same page with your partner and caregivers. I once worked with a family in New York that had three girls, a mother and father who went to work and Auntie – the mother's sister, who looked after the girls. The mother complained that her kids didn't listen to her and I soon realised she had not put boundaries and house rules in place. We worked on creating their expectations together and communicated them to the kids and to Auntie so that everybody was on the same page. But when the parents left for the day, Auntie would create her own rules because she felt that when she was babysitting, she had the right to do what she wanted. The girls were totally torn and confused by two family members fighting over house rules. The mother and the father felt emotionally blackmailed because they had nobody else to look after their children. Despite their fears of not being able to get other child care, they told Auntie that unless she abided by their rules, she couldn't watch the children. When she realised that they spoke with conviction, she agreed and the conflict was resolved.

4. Be a Good Role Model

In order to teach children how to have respect for themselves and others, you need to practise what you preach. Much of a child's behaviour is shaped not by what we say but by what we do. They are watching and imitating. It really is 'monkey see, monkey do' in these early years.

So if you want your children to be well-mannered, make sure you're well-mannered. Say 'excuse me', 'please' and 'thank you'; ask before taking something. If you want them to be kind, you need to act kindly. If you don't do as you say, you really can't

**KNOW HOW:
TEACHING EMPATHY**

Empathy is an incredibly important aspect of emotional intelligence that must be taught. You can start at around age two to help your child consider and care about other people's feelings:

• Point out how someone else might feel – 'Look, he hit his knee. That must feel bad. Let's go see how he is. How shall we make it better?'

• When she does something kind, point it out. Perhaps she shared a toy with her younger sister and you say, 'That was really kind of you.' She won't know what 'kind' is, but when you use the word she'll relate it to the action. Use a caring tone of voice.

• Empathy is an awareness that won't fully kick in till around age five, but if you keep at it, he will care about and for others by the time he starts school.

expect anything different from your kids. It's hypocritical, confusing and contradictory.

5. Praise and Reward When He Does It Right

Praise is *such* an important part of shaping positive behaviour. By acknowledging what he did right and showing happiness about a particular behaviour, you are teaching him to keep on doing it. I can't overemphasise the importance of praise. It actually creates an upward spiral of good behaviour. He does something right; you say,

'That's wonderful that you played nicely with your sister'; he does it more to make you happy; you praise more; he does it even more.

This positive cycle works because fundamentally toddlers *want* to please you. They don't wake up thinking, 'Today I'm really going to annoy Mummy and Daddy and do the opposite of whatever they say.' They actually want to make you happy. They want to please because they want approval. The more you approve of their behaviour, the more good behaviour they give you to keep you pleased.

How you praise matters. It's more than 'Good job' or 'Well done.' Instead you need to use what I call descriptive praise, which is saying what you saw him do and why it's a good thing: 'I noticed you put your book away. That's great! That way you can find it next time.' That sort of description helps your child's brain learn not only *what* to do but *why*. It helps him know what to do next time.

I've always been a big advocate of praise and recently brain scientists have unlocked the secret of why it's so important. When someone receives descriptive praise, her brain gets a hit of the feel-good hormone dopamine, which makes her feel happy. So her brain makes the connection that if she does more of what she just got praised for, she'll feel good again.

Unfortunately, parents can get caught up in a negative spiral when dealing with their toddler's behaviour. They can be so focused on what she's doing wrong that they can't even see what she's doing right. All they do is discipline – it's the Naughty Step every hour.

If you find yourself in those circumstances, you've got to give your child a step up on the positive ladder by pointing out when you *didn't* see the negative behaviour. For instance, if over the last two weeks she's been always fighting over toys and then you notice she isn't, that's when you have to jump in: 'I noticed that you played really well with your friend today and shared your toys. I'm proud of you. It made playing more fun.'

This is *so* important. In order to build positive behaviour, you must change the glasses you've been looking at your child through and give her positive praise when you see, even for a moment, the behaviour you want or the absence of the behaviour you don't want: 'I like this behaviour right now.' 'This is what I like to see from you.'

That's going to be challenging for a lot of parents, especially if you've been used to seeing the negatives. Do you praise descriptively and make an effort in acknowledging your children's progress at least ten times a day, no matter if it's the smallest of things? I promise you it will make a huge difference in creating the behaviour you want to see. It doesn't have to be only in words. You can show them physically as well with a smile or a hug. I once worked with a very large family where the mum made big red hearts and gave them out before dinner, praising each child specifically for something he or she had done that day. The kids looked forward to it every evening.

Can you honestly say you praise your child enough? Here's how you can tell: Does it feel awkward? Because if it does, it means you don't do it enough. If so, make a conscious decision to praise more.

In addition to verbal praise and hugs, I also do believe in reward systems like jars (where you put in a ball when he correctly does what you're working on and then gets a small reward when he gets

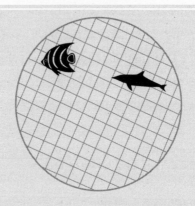

HOW TO MAKE A REWARD CHART

- Pick a theme your child is into right now – fish, for instance.

- Cut out pictures of ten different kinds of fish and draw a big fishing net out of cardboard. Or actually attach a net to the cardboard.

- Each time he does what he's supposed to, he gets to stick a fish onto the net using tape, or he can put the fish in the net.

- When he gets to ten fish, he gets a small reward.

to ten balls in the jar) and reward charts (see box on next page on how to make a reward chart). Many a time on TV you've seen me make a reward chart. I use such things when I want a child to visually track the progress he's making. He wants to behave well so he can interact with the chart. It can also help you keep your perspective that progress is being made. For those of you with smart phones, look for my reward chart app.

I remember a little boy I worked with in California who was having trouble eating a variety of foods. So I created a cherry tree chart out of felt. The cherries were in a little bucket and he would take a cherry out of the bucket and put it on the tree when he ate what he was served. When the cherries were all on the tree, his reward was to be able to ride his bike around the block with his dad, which he loved to do.

6. Comment When You See Others Do It

Another way to reinforce positive behaviour is to point it out when you see others doing it. Of course he's watching your behaviour. But you can comment when other people are behaving nicely as well: 'See how the little boy is letting you play with his train?' And show the effect: 'That way everyone can have a turn.' This helps him see the good behaviour around him and to learn from all the experiences he's having.

Be careful when you do this not to use it to shame him: 'Why can't you be like that little boy?' Whatever you do, don't compare. Just point out the behaviour you want to see: 'Look at how nicely that girl is putting her toys away before she leaves.'

7. Do It Every Day

What you are doing here is training your child to behave acceptably, appropriately and respectfully. This takes years and years. It's not a week's worth of doing it or a month's worth of doing it.

It's just like eating. You're going to say, 'Say "please"' a thousand times. You're going to have to prompt sharing a hundred or more times. You are going to need to praise him for anything you see him doing right many times a day. That's why it takes discipline on your part – the willingness to persist, to be consistent, to be patient, to keep your sense of humour about it. You *have* to be on top of it daily. And if you've slacked off for a while, get back on the horse as soon as possible. Remember what an honour you have in raising a decent child who will grow into an adult who will take her place in this world.

8. Have Consequences for Inappropriate Behaviour

In *every* household that I have gone into where there's been misbehaviour, there have been no real consequences for inappropriate behaviour. You can shape all the positive behaviour you want, but if you don't have consequences for the negative, you are operating with only half of what's needed. What happens when she pushes the boundaries, steps over the line? You tell her to stop, but what if she doesn't? A child will continue to misbehave if there's no impact on her for that behaviour. It's as simple as that. That's why you must be a disciplinarian. In Chapter 13, I go into detail about appropriate consequences for this age group and how to put them in place.

THIRTEEN

Good Behaviour SOS

You understand the importance of discipline, have become clear on your rules and boundaries and made your expectations clear to your child. Now what do you actually do when your child misbehaves?

This chapter focuses on the SOS of naughty behaviour. My definition of naughty behaviour is unacceptable, defiant behaviour. You've been clear about a house rule and your child knowingly chooses to violate that rule. He hits or throws when you've told him not to. He climbs up on the kitchen countertops even though he's been told not to. You tell your five-year-old not to run through the clothes at Target and he says, 'Okay, Mummy,' and then as soon as your back is turned, he does it again. In each of these situations, you've been clear about what's expected and he chose to defy you. That's naughty behaviour because he's not doing as he was told.

A note on the word *naughty*. We use it to descote unacceptable behaviour. I use it purposely to explain a particular behaviour to a child: 'That's naughty.' I'm not saying the *child* is bad; I am saying *what she's done* is bad. And she needs to know that. I don't want parents to feel like they can't ever use the word *naughty*.

When you start to take control of misbehaviour, toddlers often throw a tantrum: shouting, throwing themselves on the floor, stamping their feet, crossing their arms. They all do it similarly – it's as if they've all read the same 'how to throw a tantrum' book. I make a distinction between tantrums and naughty behaviour and believe they need to be handled differently. Part III outlines the three kinds of tantrums and how to deal with each so you will know how to respond correctly when a tantrum occurs. This chapter will focus on what discipline techniques to use when your child misbehaves.

Combined with my techniques, the SOS method is crucially important to use with misbehaviour because it's so easy for parents to get emotionally triggered themselves when children act up. It can be shocking when your little one throws sand in another toddler's face or bites someone. It can be upsetting when he won't do as you say and stomps off. And it can be frustrating to deal with the same issue day after day. When a child is misbehaving, you can feel out of control. You just want his behaviour to stop and it's exhausting to deal with over and over.

Remember, the Step Back helps you keep your cool – it brings clarity and focus so that you can think logically about the situation and implement the appropriate consequence in a calm, disciplined manner. Being disciplined in your approach is essential because one of the most common mistakes parents make in discipline is inconsistency – not following the Naughty Step technique precisely, for instance, and/or not following through with a consequence every time.

When you Observe, make sure you are focusing on what you

COMMON DISCIPLINE MISTAKES PARENTS MAKE

- Warn but don't follow through. Your kids quickly learn they don't have to take you seriously.

- Lack of consistency. If something's not acceptable one day, it shouldn't be acceptable another. It doesn't matter if you don't feel like following through on a consequence or if it's an inconvenient time or place.

- Impatience with the technique – 'I did it once and it didn't work so I'm stopping.' Her misbehaviour has likely gone on for a while, so it will take time for her to learn you mean business and for you to master the technique.

---

are seeing. Of course you don't like the behaviour. But focus on what he is actually doing. Then Step In with a consequence to help your child recognise that he must listen to what you're asking and be responsible for his behaviour. Step In as a conscious parent and discipline, knowing you're taking control of the situation so that his behaviour will get better as he gets older and understands more.

DISCIPLINE UNDER AGE TWO

Your fifteen-month-old has started biting you when she gets angry or frustrated. You're not sure what sort of discipline, if any, is appropriate at this age. When it happens, it really hurts!

Step Back: Take a breath and don't react.

Observe: When does it happen? What is setting it off? Is she teething? What do you do in response? Do you just ignore it or do you tell her no?

What do you want to achieve? Your child learning not to bite.

DEALING WITH UNDER-TWO MISBEHAVIOURS

- Biting, hitting, taking someone's toys – kids this age do these things to get a reaction from you. If you respond strongly, they will do it again. So be as casual as possible.

- If he's taken someone else's toy, just give it back and distract him with something else.

- If he bites or hits you when you are holding him, say, 'No, owie, that hurts,' then put him down a few feet away from you for a few minutes. When he comes back over to you, pick him up and say, 'Owie, that hurt. Give Mummy a kiss.' 'No more or Mummy will put you down again.'

- If he bites or hits anyone else, remove him from their space and say a similar thing.

- Praise him for not biting or hitting when he's behaving nicely: 'That's good, no bite [hit].'

Step In: Biting is usually an act of anger or frustration that occurs with children who don't yet have the language to express themselves in words. However, you can also see biting when a child is teething, which would mean that she may be in discomfort and needs pain relief.

If you see she's biting from anger or frustration, put her down away from you. She is too young for the Naughty Step, as she doesn't yet have the capacity to understand rules, warnings and consequences. That doesn't mean you can't begin to teach her that it is not okay. When she bites you, follow the instructions in the 'Dealing with Under-Two Misbehaviours' box on page 216. Be consistent and she'll soon learn through repetition not to do it.

HAVEN'T BEEN EFFECTIVELY DISCIPLINING

You don't live with your five-year-old's mother and only see him on weekends. So when you are together, you don't want to spoil the experience by disciplining him. He's got really out of control, not listening to anything you tell him and you know you should be doing something.

Step Back: Take a breath and don't react.

Observe: What effects do you see as a result of no discipline? Does your child respect and listen to you? Take direction so you can feel safe about going outside? As time goes on, is his behaviour getting worse? What are your beliefs about discipline – that if you have rules and consequences your child won't love you?

What do you want to achieve? Having your child listen to you.

Step In: I call dads in this situation 'Disney dads' because they tend to want to be the hero in their kids' eyes and take them on all kinds of exciting adventures. There's nothing wrong with that, but it has to be balanced with discipline. Your child is crying out for you to take control. You have to set your feelings of guilt aside and really understand that your son needs discipline, just like he needs food and sleep. I see the same kind of problem with working mothers who don't want to discipline when they come home in the evening because they feel guilty about being gone all day.

How you feel is secondary to what your child needs from you. While it may not be pleasant to be a disciplinarian, you'll find that it will not drive a wedge between you; rather, it will allow you to have more fun in the long run because you won't be trying to get him to listen to you all the time.

The good news is that it's not going to take you ages to turn the situation around if you are consistent. Start by making your rules clear. Then use the Naughty Step technique when he defies a rule. I suggest the Naughty Step because he is old enough to understand. It's my generally preferred method of discipline for children over two because it is so immediate. Whether you use a chair, a mat or a stair step doesn't matter. Just have a designated place in your home where he is to stay so he can begin to understand the difference between right and wrong behaviour.

THE NAUGHTY STEP TECHNIQUE

1. Before you need it, designate a spot in your house.
2. If he misbehaves, give a warning in a low-toned,

authoritative voice, make eye contact and make sure you are at the child's height so as not to intimidate. This gives him a chance to self-correct.

3. If he ignores the warning, take him to the step and explain why he's there: 'You have to sit here because we don't hit.' If you choose to, tell him how long he's going to be on the step.

4. Walk away and set a timer for one minute per year of age. You walk away so that *you* remain composed and so that there can be no conversation or power play on his part.

5. He will most likely try to get up, at least at first. If he gets up, you put him back and reset the timer. Do this again and again if necessary until he can sit there for the length of time you have set. Remember, no talking to your child at this stage.

6. Consistently putting him back sends a very strong message that you mean what you say and are following through. Your job is to stay calm and consistent no matter how many times you have to put him on the spot. What's most important is that you are in control of this situation. You know that if he gets up, you are going to put him back. Make sure you do it silently and be aware of your body language. I've watched parents strain their eyeballs indicating 'get back' and have watched arms point to the Naughty Step as if they were danger signs on railway tracks. Just put him back.

7. Your child may get off the step and look to play what I call 'cat and mouse', waiting for you to run and place him

back over again. Ignore that if he runs back to the spot when you approach. He's already put himself back. Simply reset the timer.

8. When the timer goes off, go back and say, 'Okay, time's up.' Explain again why he was put there, because when children are very young, they're learning to remember.

9. Ask him to apologise. The apology is very important, as it helps your child take responsibility for his actions and helps him start to learn how to redeem himself when he does something inappropriate.

10. Once he's apologised, give hugs and kisses, which show that you are not holding any personal grudge, but merely teaching him the importance of respecting the behaviour required and the concept of consequences.

NOT SHARING SPACE WITH OTHERS

When you go to a bouncy castle or on the slide at the playground, your three-year-old hogs the space. He physically uses his body to keep others out and sometimes even screams or cries if another child comes near. You've talked to him about sharing and taking turns and practised a lot at home, but it's not translating into good behaviour in public. You are so embarrassed in front of the other parents.

Step Back: Take a breath and don't react.

Observe: In addition to teaching him to share space, have you made it clear that this is naughty behaviour? Because of your embarrassment, how do you behave? Have you issued a warning and followed through with a consequence?

What do you want to achieve? Your child playing nicely in public spaces and having fun with other kids.

Step In: He needs to know this is unacceptable. You need to nip this in the bud or it could easily turn into bullying behaviour. Continue to practise taking turns at home. Remind him of how he should behave whenever you are about to go into a situation where this might occur. Then use my Sideline technique if necessary (see below). The Sideline technique is good for young children because you exclude them from the action they want to be part of, so the consequence is clear and they see how other children are behaving nicely, which prompts good behaviour. Make sure when he's sitting out that he doesn't have anything else to play with. The point is to feel left out and bored!

As for your own feelings, don't let them get in the way. You don't need to make excuses about why he's behaving like this. Simply say 'Excuse me, I'm going to go over and help my son learn to share space' and smile. Then get on with it. Likely the other parents will appreciate your handling it! Remember, most kids will do this – they live in their own bubble, where everything is 'mine'.

THE SIDELINE TECHNIQUE

1. Remind him about proper behaviour – to share what he has, take turns, not hit.

2. If he doesn't behave, walk him to the sideline of the activity so he can see everybody else getting along and having fun.

3. Say, 'You know what? You didn't share [you didn't take turns, you hit], so now you'll have to sit out for a little while. You can go back and join in when you can do it better.'

4. Keep him out for a couple of minutes, just long enough for him to get the point. Explain before he goes back to play, 'If you want to play, you have to share [take turns, not hit].'

5. Your tone of voice should be firm but fair.

FIGHTING OVER TOYS

Your three- and four-year-olds are constantly fighting over their toys and games. You've worked on sharing and taking turns, but the battles continues. They break and throw things and generally create mayhem in their room.

Step Back: Take a breath and don't react.

Observe: What is actually going on? Is one the instigator who tends to grab from the other? Or is it more of a matter of them not respecting their toys – strewing them around the room, stepping on them, throwing them down in anger? Can they share and take turns in other settings, such as on playdates and the playground?

What do you want to achieve? Your children learning to treat their things nicely and play well together.

Step In: In situations like this, you may need to work more on sharing and taking turns even though you feel like you've done it over and over. These social skills can take a long time to become habit – meaning this situation is not solved in a week.

As for discipline, I would suggest using my Confiscation Box technique (see below), where you take away the toy they were fighting over for a while. This generally sends the message loud and clear, because even though kids have lots of toys, they want the one that's been taken away. But do also pay attention to the dynamic between the two. If one is generally bullying the other by grabbing toys away, then you will need to use the Naughty Step to teach her to treat her sister more kindly. And remember – it isn't always the older one who is dominant, particularly when they are so close in age. Give them chances to play alone and to respect each other's space.

Here's another way to teach young ones to respect belongings. I helped a family in Chicago where the boys had a beautiful downstairs area to play. But their toys were scattered all over. It made life a nightmare for the mum, who had to try to find puzzle and game pieces. So I had each of them choose ten toys they wanted to play with. Those went in a box. Then I took all the other toys and put them out of reach in the garage. Gradually, through better behaviour, they earned back their other toys.

THE CONFISCATION BOX TECHNIQUE

1. If, after a warning, your child is still misbehaving, take the toy, put it into a box and place the box where he can't reach it.

2. When he complains, explain, 'Respect your toys or lose
   them.' The length of time you keep the toy away depends
   on how old he is and what he's done. I would give a
   three- or four-year-old one day to make the point and
   two days if it happens again. Then stick with that. This
   technique doesn't really work with one- or two-year-
   olds, as they don't have the cognitive ability to understand
   what you are doing.

3. Don't buy him a new toy for good behaviour. That sends
   the message that no matter how many toys you confis-
   cate, he can get more, so it defeats the purpose of the
   technique.

BEING DISRESPECTFUL

*Your son turned four and suddenly you are seeing a lot of cheeky
behaviour. Yesterday when you were out, you told him politely it
was time to go and he told you to shut up. You told him that this
is not acceptable, but he continued to be disrespectful, saying he
didn't have to listen to you. You're not sure what discipline is best
in this situation.*

Step Back: Take a breath and don't react.

Observe: Were you in a place where you could do the Naughty
Step? Or were you in a situation where it would be inconvenient
to do it? If the latter is true, what kinds of fun things were you
planning to do the rest of the day?

What do you want to achieve? The understanding that it is unacceptable to talk with a cheeky manner, period.

Step In: My suggestion in this circumstance would be to use the Loss of Privilege technique. (See below.) It works well with an older toddler, say four or five, who can understand the concept of a consequence that happens later.

Make sure that what he loses is something he enjoys doing, so that he will feel the consequence of his behaviour. His sense of disappointment will help him become more mindful of the impact of what he is doing. Praise the positive behaviour you start to see and don't forget to lead by example.

THE LOSS OF PRIVILEGE TECHNIQUE

1. Think about something your child likes to do that she's been looking forward to – maybe going to the park or riding her bike. This needs to be based on your child's likes.
2. If she acts up, give a warning: 'If you don't stop this right now, you will not get to ride your bike this afternoon.'
3. If she continues to misbehave, say, 'Okay, no bike for you this afternoon.'
4. When the time comes, remind her that she cannot do it because she misbehaved. Because it's something she likes to do, she'll think, 'That didn't feel good. I don't want to have that happen to me again, so I'm going to listen next time.'

DISCIPLINE NOT WORKING

You've been using the Naughty Step technique with your two-and-a-half-year-old, but you don't think it's working. When she does something wrong, you put her there for two minutes and she laughs the whole time. As soon as she gets up, she does the same thing again and ends up back on the step. This can go on for a long time.

Step Back: Take a breath and don't react.

Observe: Are you following every step of the technique exactly? Do you give a warning first? Is she a very strong-willed child, so she's testing you to see if you really mean it? What is she getting in trouble for? Could it be that you need to be helping her more with early learning so that she can do as she's told? What time of the day does this happen? How are her sleep and eating routines? What happens to you when she laughs? Do you give up?

What do you want to achieve? Your child doing what she's told.

Step In: Ignore her laughing – she's trying to defuse your emotions so you will give up. Make sure that you are following each step, including giving a warning and reinforcing what she did wrong at the end: 'You hit the dog and that hurt her. That's naughty behaviour.' You want to make sure she is learning. If she does it again, start over. She's likely testing you to see if you really follow through.

Make sure you have the four other basics in place – that she's getting adequate sleep, food, stimulation and outside adventures. Think about what you need to teach her so she doesn't keep getting into trouble. Does she need help following directions? Sharing? Listening? When parents tell me that discipline isn't working, it is usually because they are not following the steps exactly or aren't providing the right other basics so that their child can do what they're asking of her. Remember, your love, affection and descriptive praise will make her want to gain your approval and feel good about pleasing you.

ACTING UP IN PUBLIC

You don't know why, but your two-and-a-half-year-old daughter seems to act much worse out in public than at home. She screams 'no' and hits you when you tell her to do something, such as get into the buggy when it's time to leave the park or not touch things in the shop. You get flustered because you feel people are looking at you and you aren't sure of the right way to handle the situation.

Step Back: Take a breath and don't react.

Observe: What do you do when she hits? Do you have consequences? Do you ever give in and let her have her way because you are embarrassed? What is your emotional state – calm or upset?

What do you want to achieve? Your child doing as she's told in public.

Step In: In this situation, the Step Back is very important, because the number one thing you need to do to turn this around is to stay calm and matter-of-fact while dealing consistently with her naughty behaviour. That's because at some point in their development, toddlers begin to understand that if they do certain things, it will get a rise out of you. That's why she's acting up in public – she sees your embarrassment and knows that you are more likely to give in on whatever it is she wants. So your job is to not give in no matter what. Use the Naughty Step technique if she misbehaves – use a bench or log or patch of lawn – and congratulate yourself for having the discipline to deal with the situation rather than letting your embarrassment keep you from acting. Also use the Speaking Clock technique (page 252) to improve her behaviour.

KIDS WON'T LISTEN

You have three kids under the age of five and it feels like they rule the roost. One or another is always misbehaving and you find yourself yelling, 'If you don't stop that right now, you are going to be in trouble!' all day long. It's got so you hate to take them anywhere because you don't trust that they will listen to you. Your husband doesn't have this problem at all – they do what he says when he says it. But he's only at home at night.

Step Back: Take a breath and don't react.

Observe: Is yelling your (ineffective) form of discipline? What exactly are your children doing that must be disciplined? Do you have consequences for misbehaviour? Do you issue an *effective* warning? Do you follow through and put the consequence in place after you give a warning? Are you consistent every time there is misbehaviour or do you 'pick your battles' and sometimes ignore the behaviour because you're tired?

What do you want to achieve? Your children respecting you.

Step In: If you find yourself in this circumstance, you need a very firm plan of action and you need one now. They know how to listen – they do so with Daddy. But you've taught them they don't have to listen to you. Because you've had no consequences or follow-through, you are going to have to be extremely disciplined because you've underestimated yourself. Here's my step-by-step plan to turn this situation around:

- Think about what you are constantly yelling about and turn your complaints into rules. Explain the rules to your children.
- When someone breaks a rule, issue a warning. (See next page.)
- Warn once, then follow through with the Naughty Step. If you don't follow through, then it shows that what you are asking is not that important to you and your child doesn't have to listen.
- Don't 'pick your battles'. If you are dealing with defiant behaviour, you need to be consistent whether you are at home or away, no matter the circumstances. If it's wrong, it's wrong, period. You may choose which battle to focus on first, but that doesn't mean you ignore the rest. And yes, you can discipline more than one child at once. I've had triplets on three Naughty Steps. If that's too hard for you, do it one at a time.

- Follow each step exactly. You may have to put a child back on the Naughty Step many times at first. And remember the other half of the coin – acknowledge and praise good behaviour.

Warning Dos and Don'ts

A warning is very important in discipline because it lets your child know he's exhibiting undesirable behaviour and gives him the chance to change. Here are my dos and don'ts:

Do come down to his level, two to three feet away and make eye contact so you have his full attention.

Do use an assertive tone of voice (low, firm) to express your displeasure and disapproval. It sends the signal that this is not an ordinary conversation.

Do speak slowly and very precisely so he understands what you are saying: 'Do not hit her again. That's naughty.'

Do walk away then, to allow him to show you that he's going to make the right choice and behave.

Don't issue a warning more than once: 'I really mean it – if you do it again, you will be in trouble.' 'I'm going to count to three . . . one . . . two . . .'

Don't fail to follow through if he doesn't listen to the warning: 'Okay, you can go back to play this time, but listen to me next time.'

DOES YOUR CHILD *REALLY* HATE YOU?

When you set limits or discipline your almost-five-year-old, she says, 'I hate you', You can't believe how much it hurts. Does she really mean it? You don't like to admit it, but you've started to avoid disciplining her because you don't want her to say it.

Step Back: Take a breath and don't react.

Observe: Why do you think she's saying it? In addition to discipline, are you giving her lots of love and affection? Descriptive praise when she does things well? Does she also say 'I love you' sometimes? Hug you spontaneously? What would be the ultimate outcome if you gave in and stopped disciplining her altogether?

What do you want to achieve? Teaching her how to behave.

Step In: Kids will pull every trick in the book to get what they want. And they are incredibly good at knowing just what will get parents upset. That's why, when you Step In to deal with naughty behaviour, you must have a plan to do what you need to, even though you don't want to. Back in the day they called it 'tough love'. Think about it – *tough* really means 'strong, unbreakable, dependable.' In that sense real love *is* tough love.

Keep in mind what you are trying to achieve. Put your feelings aside. Remember that for a young child, 'I hate you' means 'I'm angry with you in this moment'. In addition to implementing discipline, find lots of ways to have fun together and to tell her how much you appreciate her when she does things right.

CONSTANTLY RESISTING YOU

It seems like your two-and-a-half-year-old spends most of her day on the Naughty Step because she fights you on everything from getting dressed in the morning to going to bed at night. You pray this is just a phase – not only is it really unpleasant, but you're afraid she may have Oppositional Defiant Disorder.

Step Back: Take a breath and don't react.

Observe: Are you using the Naughty Step as a way to totally control your child? Do you make time for fun and going at her own pace or do you run your schedule with military precision? What's your tone of voice when you speak to her – is it very stern and harsh? Or do you speak more cooperatively, like, 'Let's go up-stairs now because it's bath time'? Do you let her know what you are going to do next so that she has time to transition? Do you allow her reasonable choices – which shirt to put on, which of two cereals she'd like – or are you dictating everything? Are you giving her the opportunities for independence toddlers need by teaching her life skills and letting her do things such as getting dressed by herself?

What do you want to achieve? A child who is happy and well behaved.

Step In: What I've seen with many parents is that once they've mastered the Naughty Step technique, they use it to *control* their child. They become very much like a drill sergeant: 'Go sit at the table and if you don't do it straightaway, you'll be on the Naughty Step!' There's no transition between the thing the child is doing

OPPOSITIONAL DEFIANT DISORDER

This is a condition that is characterised by, among other things:

1. Refusing to comply with adult requests

2. Deliberately annoying other people

3. Expressing anger and resentment

4. Blaming others for own mistakes

5. Seeking revenge

6. Being easily annoyed

7. Having excessive tantrums

Like with ADHD, these characteristics are very common in the toddler years. By age four or five most children start to be more cooperative and compliant. See your doctor if you are concerned.

and the parent's demand. It's as if you were on the computer writing an email and I just came over and pulled the plug because it was time for dinner. There's no respect for the other person's rhythm or timing.

Parents like this are too authoritarian, which means they also don't allow their child choices or the chance to experience independence. That's why you see constant battles – she's fighting you for the right to have some say over what she does and when and how she does it. This push for independence is a natural, healthy part of toddler development that some parents fight against because they have a strong need to control.

I'm not saying you should give a two-year-old free rein. But when you really observe the situation, you may indeed discover that you're being controlling and your child is crying out for freedom. If this seems true, try lightening your tone of voice. Offer choices: 'Do you want the blue one or the red one?' Give her a chance to do some things the way she wants to do them. Give her advance notice that she needs to move from one activity to another. Use descriptive praise when she does things well. No child should be on the Naughty Step all day! And if she is, you are definitely missing some things you should be doing.

Finally, if indeed your child has Oppositional Defiant Disorder (see box on page 233), allowing some freedom of choice and positively reinforcing the behaviour you want to see will help.

WHINING

Your son just turned three and suddenly, like a switch being flipped, he began whining over everything. It's absolutely driving you crazy and you just want it to stop! What should you do?

Step Back: Take a breath and don't react.

Observe: When does he whine – when he's tired? Hungry? Feeling overwhelmed? What do you do when he whines? Do you respond to him? Ignore him? Tell him to stop whining?

What do you want to achieve? His speaking in a normal tone.

Step In: You don't need research to tell you that whining is one of the most distracting sounds in the world – but studies have confirmed just that. It often shows up at around age three and is certainly one of the most annoying toddler behaviours parents face. Knowing why he's whining can help you address the underlying need, but often a child whines for no apparent reason so don't stress if you can't figure out why at any given moment.

Your game plan has two steps to stop this tone as quickly as possible. First, you have to teach him what whining is. When he does it, say, 'Use your proper voice, not like this . . .' and then mimic back, in a humorous way, how he sounds. Then ask him again to use his proper voice. This will help him learn the difference.

Step two is to *never* respond to what he's asking for until he says it properly. That way you are rewarding him for using the right tone, not the wrong one. Otherwise this whining phase can go on for years, as you have taught him it will get him what he wants.

DEFIANCE?

You ask your two-year-old to sit down and to eat his lunch. He's really a well-behaved child in general, but he keeps getting up from the table. Every time you put him back, he sits there for a short bit, smiling and looking happy and then gets down again. You wonder if you should be putting him on the Naughty Step so that he will learn to sit down and eat.

Step Back: Take a breath and don't react.
Observe: Does he seem like he is being defiant or is it that he has not been taught to sit down for an extended period of time?

Have you worked on expanding his sitting time? How long can he sit doing anything?

What do you want to achieve? Having him be able to sit down for a whole meal and be engaged.

Step In: There is a difference between a child being defiant and one who doesn't know how to do what is required. The clues here for me in this scenario are that he's generally well behaved and he's smiling and looking happy rather than having that sullen face that says, 'I don't want to do what you're saying and I'm not going to.' What this means to me is that he really needs support with his early learning skills of attention span, focus and concentration.

This is an important distinction. It's not fair to discipline a child for something that he can't help doing because it's above his developmental level or he hasn't been taught to do it. You *have to put in place* everything in the other four categories in order to know that you can in good conscience implement discipline.

CUTTING SOME SLACK BECAUSE OF CIRCUMSTANCES

Your four-year-old is having a really tough time. Her beloved dog died and she's had to go to a new day care place. As a result, you are seeing a lot more acting out. She seems to have regressed back to a three-year-old – screaming and hitting when she doesn't get her way, refusing to share, throwing things . . . The day care place called to complain and you told them to cut her some slack because of all she's going through. That's what you've been doing too.

Step Back: Take a breath and don't react.

Observe: What's going on emotionally? Do you believe that any behaviour is excusable? If it's okay to cut her some slack, when do you decide to discipline her again? What are you teaching her by letting her behave this way?

What do you want to achieve? Proper behaviour towards other people.

Step In: When your child is going through something very difficult, it is natural to want to make things as easy as possible. You can do that by giving her lots of cuddle time with you and chances to talk about how she's feeling. However, that doesn't mean it's okay for her to hurt someone else. Even death has boundaries. You cannot stop correcting bad behaviour because of her emotional circumstances. She has to learn that certain behaviours are not acceptable no matter how she feels. Otherwise you are being too indulgent.

In these circumstances, I would use the Sideline technique (see page 221) and ask her to apologise to the other person. In addition, at other times of the day, show her lots of empathy; comfort her with words, affection and reassurances so that she may heal.

PART 3

Taming
Tantrums

FOURTEEN

The Three Types of Tantrums

Every parent has experienced the shock of that moment when their sweet baby turns into a tantruming toddler: kicking, shrieking, throwing herself down on the ground. Good God, it's overwhelming, not to mention the noise. It can stir up all kinds of out-of-control feelings in you: anger, shame, embarrassment, inadequacy and fear. You want the tantrum to stop instantly and never happen again. You get angry at yourself and/or your child when you can't stop it. You feel out of control and worry about your lack of control. You're afraid your little darling has turned into a nightmare. You worry that you are a bad parent. Why on earth would she be behaving like this if you weren't? And how long is it going to last?

It's bad enough if the two of you are at home alone, but she doesn't do it just at home. In the park, at the supermarket, at family gatherings . . . and why is it that tantrums seem to happen especially when you want her to be on her best behaviour so you can impress your friends and relatives with how well behaved she is? Now, on top of having to deal with an out-of-control child, you're also worried about other people judging your parenting abilities.

Dealing effectively with tantrums begins with understanding what they are and why they occur. That's what this chapter is all about. I can hear you saying 'finally!' Then, in Chapter 15, I will help you apply my SOS technique in order to effectively handle them in the moment with as little emotional toll on you and your child as possible no matter where and when they occur.

When babies are around eighteen months or so, they begin to experience a whirlwind of intense, contradictory and sometimes explosive emotions that they don't have words for and can't control. Such emotions combined with a toddler's developmental push for independence result in the explosions we commonly know as tantrums. They are universal; no parent escapes them. That's because they are a normal part of child development. They usually peak at age two or three and disappear over time by four or five if they are handled properly.

As someone who has put herself in the eye of the tantruming tornado thousands of times, I have discovered that there are three types of tantrums:

1. *the emotional meltdown,* which is when a toddler gets overwhelmed by feelings of sadness, hurt, excitement or fear and just 'loses it'.

TOP TEN TANTRUM TRIGGERS

1. Tiredness

2. Hunger

3. Over or under stimulation

4. Too many demands, like sharing

5. Want to do it by themselves but not being able to

6. Disputes over food

7. Emotions like fear and anxiety

8. Perfectionist temperament

9. Not getting their own way

10. New environments

2. *the situation tantrum,* which comes from getting angry or frustrated about a particular situation, such as having to sit still for too long or being unable to do something she wants to.

3. *the mock tantrum,* which is manipulative behaviour that starts to occur when you give in to situation tantrums.

Tantrums can go on for years if not handled effectively. Each needs to be dealt with differently. However, in general, parents don't know that there are three distinct types. They think they're all the same. Well, I'm here to tell you that they are different. And if you can identify which your child is having and respond appropriately, you can significantly diminish their occurrence.

Will you be able to end tantrums completely? It depends on the kind. You can end mock tantrums through your response. But no parent can completely keep emotional meltdowns and situation tantrums at bay because your child hasn't yet developed the maturity to regulate her emotions or the self-discipline to be less impulsive. However, this phase can pass very quickly when you know how to spot tantrums before they occur, respond effectively and minimise their frequency by putting in place the fundamentals that I discussed in Part II.

EMOTIONAL MELTDOWNS

Emotional meltdowns are raw expressions of upset, fear, anxiety, hurt, sadness or grief. What causes them is different for each child, but what they have in common is that your young one has been overcome with emotions and cries wildly. This tantrum could be triggered by the loss of a pet, being upset because her brother took her toy, going to nursery for two weeks and still feeling the separation from Mummy, recovering from being sick or a new baby arriving in the family. Emotionally she's having a tough time and there should be more empathy on your part with this type of tantrum.

While the sound of an emotional meltdown can be upsetting or even frightening to parents, children in these circumstances are simply trying to process their emotions in the only way they can – nonverbally. They don't yet have the ability to identify their feelings or to control them. These emotional skills have to be taught, which is why you will see in the next chapter that part of my suggestion on how to deal with emotional meltdowns is to put into words the feelings your child is experiencing. She won't be able to do it herself for years, but you will be helping her grow her emotional intelligence.

Parents need to understand that emotional meltdowns are natural, particularly under stressful circumstances. You don't want to suppress her feelings, but over time you can help your child learn to have more emotional control so that her feelings aren't destructive to herself or to others around her.

You can tell a true emotional meltdown because the crying is truly uncontrolled. His lip may quiver and he may pant, hiccup or shake. At some point, the crying fit starts to slow down. He may start taking short little breaths as it peters out. Afterwards, he tends to be exhausted and may fall asleep.

SITUATION TANTRUMS

As the name suggests, these are outbursts of frustration or anger because of a particular situation. It may be because he has to sit too long in the pew at the wedding. Or you're out at a restaurant and have been waiting too long for food. Or there are no more orange lollies left and only green and red to choose from. Some-one new has come through the door and he doesn't want him in the house. Whatever the triggering situation is, suddenly you have an angry child who has lost control. He may cry, scream, throw himself on the ground and generally 'lose it'.

Situation tantrums are triggered by a child's desire for inde-pendence, which begins around the age of two. She wants to pour the milk herself, but she doesn't understand the jug is too heavy. So she gets frustrated and loses control. She wants to put on her own clothes, but you are in a hurry so you are doing it instead.

A situation tantrum occurs in direct response to a particular situation your child is in. As with emotional meltdowns, it is your job to help him understand what he's feeling and why, because this will help him develop emotional self-awareness. And as with emotional meltdowns, it's a pure, uncontrolled expression of feeling. He's not trying to manipulate you; he's just expressing his frustration and anger in the only way he knows.

With a situation tantrum, you need to understand why it's happening. I see lots of parents getting angry at their kids over a situation they've put their child in! If you've run very late with dinner, if you've asked a two-year-old to sit still for an hour in church or if you haven't taken the time to teach your child how to put on his pants, then you've got to understand that your child is having this tantrum *because* of the situation. That's why SOS is so important. Once you know what's going on, you can mirror that to your child: 'I know you're tired [or frustrated or hungry].' If your child then moves on to become destructive by throwing, hitting, spitting and/or kicking, then you have to address that with a discipline technique.

But with a lot of situation tantrums, most of the learning needs to be on the parents' side: what do you need to do with the four other basic rules so you don't get into this situation again? Once you're aware of how to avoid the situation, then you'll reduce these types of tantrums by half. Part II of this book should help with that. But don't be too hard on yourself if tantrums occur anyway – sometimes things happen that are out of your control and you and your child just have to live through them. That's life.

MOCK TANTRUMS

Mock tantrums are acting out manipulations that are calculated to embarrass and humiliate you into giving in to whatever it is your child wants. This can be anything from having another biscuit to buying something in a shop to staying longer at the playdate. It often comes with the chant 'I need, I need . . .' or 'I want, I want . . .'

Mock tantrums develop when you give in to what your child is demanding in a situation tantrum and he learns that he can get his way by pitching a fit. This learning is not conscious, but it *is* deliberate and you can see it in children as young as nine months.

How can you tell a mock tantrum from a real one? The mock tantrum is a form of emotional blackmail that consists of the child doing everything he can think of, physical or verbal, to make you relent. It comes with theatrical, dramatic, overblown performances – 'I want it nooooowwww!' – accompanied by kicking or pounding or throwing himself on the ground. Unlike an emotional meltdown or situational tantrum, it's controllable – it may start and stop as your child checks to see if his performance is getting anywhere: *Is this working? Are you changing your mind?* Or he may forget for a few minutes that he's supposed to be upset and starts again as he realises you're listening. He may follow you around from room to room to continue the performance.

Giving in to mock tantrums is dangerous because a child learns very quickly that if she carries on and you relent, that's what she needs to do to get what she wants next time. And so the acting-out behaviour continues – or gets even stronger as she tries to force you to give in. Ultimately, when you don't deal effectively with mock tantrums, your child will learn to control you and others through her behaviour, making life incredibly difficult for her and everyone around her.

I've seen families where parents have given in so much to mock tantrums that they now have no control. They feel totally helpless to the point that it's destructive for the whole family. And that creates enormous amounts of resentment. It doesn't build trust or develop nurturing relationships between the child and her siblings, her parents or other family members. As the child gets older, it spills over to school, with her giving teachers and other students a hard time.

If you don't deal well with mock tantrums when children are two and three years old, you see them continuing or getting worse at six, seven and beyond. We expect such behaviour from two- and three-year-olds because we know that young children live in a bubble of 'me, me and me' and that they are learning to have more discipline. But when you see seven- and eight-year-olds stamping their feet and tantruming, you know their parents have not done their job.

Sometimes different types of tantrums overlap. You can be in a shop and know you've pushed the limit of your two-year-old's ability to be patient, so she's having a situation tantrum. Then suddenly she sees something she wants and goes into a mock tantrum to get it. You've got to understand the situation – 'She's bored with following me around, so we've got to go do something fun for her' – while not giving in by buying the thing she's pitching a mock fit over.

TANTRUMS ARE HEALTHY

Tantrums are a healthy part of a child's development through which he learns valuable life lessons. With emotional meltdowns, he is learning to freely express what he's feeling, to feel understood by another person and to receive comfort. In a situation tantrum, he's learning how to be more adaptable and accepting of the way things are. With a mock tantrum, he is learning that he can't always have his own way, to be more aware of people around him and to understand reasonable behaviour. Understanding this will hopefully help you handle each effectively, as you can now recognise what your child is meant to be learning.

TANTRUM PREVENTION

You can't prevent all tantrums from happening. But with good routines, planning and putting my basics and SOS techniques in place you can minimise a lot of situation tantrums and even some emotional meltdowns. And mock tantrums can be nipped in the bud through your consistent behaviour (see box on page 250).

You can also lessen the frequency of tantrums by adopting four powerful parenting techniques:

KNOW HOW:
MOCK TANTRUM PREVENTION

When a child is having a tantrum about something you have said no to, do not under any circumstance give in and say yes. It's as simple as that. Remain consistent or you will be teaching your child to tantrum more. And if you said no at home, you *must* say it outside as well, because they will ask outside too. No matter who's looking at you, no matter where you are, do not change the game plan. That takes discipline, but you can do it because you know why the tantrum is happening.

1. Think Before Giving an Answer

One of the ways parents unintentionally provoke tantrums is to agree to something and then change their minds. You tell him he can have something and then realise it's not a good idea. Or you let him out of the buggy when he asks and then decide it's not safe and want to put him back in. You say he can go to the park, then something gets in the way and you don't go. That makes him feel he can't trust your word. He's not old enough to understand that things change. To him, you promised something and then took it away.

To avoid these situations, when your child asks you for something, *think* before you answer! He asks, 'Can I play with the truck now?' Say, 'Wait a minute. Mummy needs to think about that.' Of course, plans sometimes have to change due to circumstances beyond your control, but thinking before you answer will minimise this flash point.

2. Set Expectations in Advance

When you are going out, make it clear what he can have or do before you get there: 'We're going to the shops and you can pick one book.' Then stick to it, no matter how much he throws a fit.

3. Tell, Don't Ask

When you want your child to do something, don't give her the chance to say no. Parents make this mistake with their toddlers all the time: 'Shall we put your trousers on now?' The children are too young to understand that this is just a way of saying, 'Put your trousers on now.' They think they're getting a choice and then you take the choice away. Make sure you tell, not ask. You can still do this nicely: 'Let's clean up these crayons and then we can go.' This simple technique can eliminate a tremendous number of tantrums.

4. Give Advance Warning

If you know your child has trouble with things such as leaving a friend's house, turning the TV off or not wanting to go somewhere, make sure you give advance warning before you head into the situation: 'When I say it's time to go, we will leave and if I see any nonsense from you, you'll go on the Naughty Step when you get home.' To help with the transition, use the Speaking Clock technique (see below). It works well with three- to five-year-olds, as they have an understanding of time.

THE SPEAKING CLOCK TECHNIQUE

1. Give clear notice: 'In five minutes we have to leave so we can . . .' This helps the child to prepare for change.
2. If he starts to play up, offer choices to move forward: 'Do you want to put your coat on or shall I?' 'Say goodbye to everyone.'
3. If he refuses to say goodbye, tell him, 'If you don't want to say goodbye, let's go!' He will know you are serious and he will either move reluctantly or say goodbye.
4. Let him know when it is down to the last minute.

Sometimes you can sense a tantrum is about to erupt. Is there anything you can do to prevent a full explosion? I think of tantrums as being like water coming to a boil in a pan. At first the water is still; then it starts to slightly bubble and then the bubbles start to surface. Eventually it's a roiling boil. If you can identify the behaviour that's like the little bubbles at the bottom and turn down the heat, then tantrums and meltdowns won't necessarily get to the surface.

To do this, you need the O of SOS most – to Observe your child. What happens just before he loses it? Perhaps he gets wound up, fidgety and agitated or really whiny. Or he won't look at you. Or he'll say the same thing over and over again. Some children will start to flush and you can see that they're starting to get hot.

Especially with a young child, when you see signs that an emotional meltdown or situation tantrum might occur, you can pick him up and distract him with something to do or something new to look at: 'Look at the birdie!' Or you can take him out of the situation before he tips over into a full-blown tantrum – leave the church or the party, take him outside, separate him from his sister, find a snack to eat. Try a bit of reasoning: 'I know you're hungry. What I want us to do is to sit down right now so we can get our food quickly.'

You can also often prevent situation tantrums if you pay attention to him at the first signs of him feeling upset or out of control and offer assistance. I remember a little girl that I was looking after who really wanted to put on her shoes. But she didn't have the fine motor skills to be able to weave the strip of Velcro through the hole and fasten it down. I could see it was only a matter of seconds before she had a blowout and threw the shoe. I could tell she was frustrated because her face started to get red and her movements were more jerky and impatient.

I said, 'Look at Jo-Jo for a moment, okay? We're going to take the shoe and put these straps through, okay? It goes like this,' and I gestured what to do. She looked at me and I could see her calm down. I showed her how to do it and then she did it.

HELPING A CHILD CALM DOWN

Parents often tell a child to 'calm down', but little ones don't know what that means. To help them:

- Say, for instance, 'You're angry. I don't want you throwing things and feeling really angry. Calm down. This behaviour is not calming down.'
- Create an Emotion Wheel with little lollipop faces showing different emotions. Tell her to point to the face that she's feeling.
- Once you see her calm, ask, 'Are you calm now?' If the answer is yes, then say, 'You are? Okay, so look at me and let's have a conversation now.' Then get down to her level, make eye contact and be clear about what you expect: 'Now you are going to pick up your toys.'

By striking the right balance between helping and letting your child do it himself, through distraction and diversion and by adapting your plans quickly when you see the warning signs, you can nip a lot of potential tantrums in the bud. But what do you do when they're in full flower? Read on.

THE BLOW OUT ANGER TECHNIQUE

This is a great thing to do with your child when a tantrum is about to erupt:

- Get down to her level face-to-face, about two feet apart and make eye contact.
- Ask her to copy you. Then breathe loudly and slowly through your nose to the count of 3 and breathe out loudly through your mouth. (You should slightly exaggerate this

exercise so she can see and hear clearly what you are doing.)

- Repeat five times, coaching her to do it with you, using your right hand to count the number of times you've done it. The focus and concentration needed to do this defuses the anger she is feeling and starts to help her have more discipline.

FIFTEEN

Tantrum SOS

Now that you understand why tantrums happen and the differences between the three types, it's time to learn what to do about them. Because tantrums are such a powerful burst of emotional display, a lot of parents get frustrated and want to control them. They get angry and/or frustrated at their child for being angry and/or frustrated. They get caught up in how they are feeling and how they believe everyone around them is judging them and their child. This is not the state in which to handle a tantrum well.

Like with naughty behaviour, you've got to be disciplined yourself when a tantrum occurs. Your child is out of control. You *have* to become the regulator – and that means regulating your own emotions so you can deal effectively with hers. If you display behaviour similar to your child's, you will be teaching her that emotional meltdowns and temper tantrums are okay. If you give in to the tantrums, you are only ensuring they will happen more frequently. And if you do nothing at all, blindly ignoring your child's acting out, she won't learn proper behaviour and she may even cause harm to someone else. This chapter will help you to not fall into any of these traps and give you all you need to handle tantrums well – for you and for your child.

Because of their nature, emotional meltdowns and situation tantrums are not dealt with in the same way as naughty behaviour, although if during a tantrum a child does something naughty – hitting, biting, throwing things – you would deal with that as you would any other naughty behaviour. Discipline and consequences are not going to reduce the frequency of tantrums. Rather, the basic approach is to treat these like a storm and let them run their course, making sure your child isn't hurting himself or anyone else and then deal with the situation that provoked the outburst.

One big mistake parents make is to try to reason with a child having a tantrum. Once it's begun, you can't talk your child out of an emotional meltdown or situation tantrum. But because of the tantrum's very nature – an out-of-control outburst – a child caught in a tantrum cannot reason. She cannot hear what you're saying, let alone see anything beyond what she wants or doesn't want. (This is not true of a mock tantrum, which is approached differently, as I will explain later.) So one of the most important things to remember when a child is having an emotional meltdown or situation tantrum is that you can't resolve the situation until she's calmed down.

That doesn't mean you don't do anything. Like all the other situations you find yourself in as a disciplined parent, you start with SOS. And this SOS is as crucial for you as for your child.

1. Step Back

As soon as you become aware that your child has lost it, Step Back. In a tantrum Step Back, you want to make sure you not only physically step back from the situation but also take a few slow, deep breaths.

Like with the Step Back for naughty behaviour, the Step Back here gives you emotional distance so that you don't get caught up in the storm. This is so very important. As you learned in Chapter 14, emotional meltdowns and situation tantrums are a result of overwhelming feelings. One person is out of control; you don't want to make it two, because that prevents you from being as effective as you need to be. Because of the intensity of your toddler's outburst, especially in a public setting when you feel judged, you can actually be triggered into a state of 'fight, flight or freeze' – a fear reaction coming from the brain that results in anger (fight), the desire to run (flight) or becoming unable to move (freeze).

During a tantrum, some parents become so scared they physically shake and want to flee (flight). Others stand by helplessly (freeze). Still others get angry and want to jump in and grab their child (fight). None of these is effective and anger in particular can be extremely dangerous. Does the feeling of being out of control make you mad or even aggressive? If so, learning to step back and calm down is even more important for you. (See box on next page.)

NO-NO: AGGRESSION

Anger can lead to aggression, including physical violence towards your child, which is absolutely unacceptable no matter the situation. Step out of the situation when you feel yourself losing it. Take slow, deep breaths and do not engage until you are calm. If you have been or feel you might be violent towards your child, you do need professional help.

Whichever of these responses is triggered in you by a tantrum – fight, flight or freeze – scientists have discovered that in this state, your problem-solving brain shuts down and your primitive brain takes over. Nothing good comes from this state of mind. Stepping back allows your thinking brain to come back online so you can deal effectively with the situation.

Stepping back during a tantrum is also crucial because tantrums are a toddler's way of trying to gain control. When you don't react immediately, you regain some control over the situation. You know you're going to deal with the tantrum, but you don't feel pressured to impulsively react. You're on your time, not his.

A tantruming child can be dangerous and much stronger than normal. I personally have had to duck and dive, been kicked in the back and been punched in the head. If your child's having a tantrum that's led to aggressive behaviour, get out of harm's way! I've seen many a parent who allows herself to be a punching bag, hoping that her child will see what he's done and be sorry for it. But he's never sorry in the moment. Afterwards, when he's calmed down, there may be remorse. But right then, during the tantrum, your child is enraged and you can end up getting hurt.

The same is true for verbal acting out. As a child gets older and more able to express himself, he might yell, scream or say things that pull on your heartstrings: 'I hate you. I know you hate me. I want another mummy.' Of course such things hurt in the moment. But I can't tell you the number of parents who ask me, 'Does he really think I hate him?' I always say to take it as an expression of how angry he was. Part of the job of being a parent is understanding the difference between the things your young ones do out of frustration and helplessness and the thoughts and feelings that exist after the heat of the moment passes. *No matter what she says during a tantrum, do not engage verbally with her. This is not a negotiation! Do not feed the tantrum.*

Another common mistake parents make with a tantruming toddler is to try to turn her around to face them during the tantrum. This only gives her a chance to hit or kick you. Some parents try to hold the child as she kicks or hits. That's like trying to control a rampaging bull. Move away. Don't approach unless she is in danger of hurting herself. Not physically getting caught

KNOW HOW:
SELF-DEFENCE TIP

If your child is trying to hit, kick, or otherwise physically hurt you, defend yourself with your arms up if necessary. In a very firm, calm voice say, 'I don't want you in my space now. I'll talk to you when you calm down.' Then walk away if it is safe to do so. If she follows, go into another room and close the door.

up in the fray will go a long way towards lessening the toll of the tantrum on you and your child.

Of course, in all situations and in every tantrum it is your obligation to make sure he's not going to harm himself. I remember very clearly being asked to babysit for a six-year-old I'd never met before. When I got there I found out that he was still being pushed in a buggy. The plan was for me to take him on a bus sightseeing around London. So naturally I wanted him to walk, which he was completely capable of doing. He pitched a big mock tantrum, trying to convince me to get the buggy. He even tried to run into the road. I had to hold him until he calmed down. We sat on the sidewalk, me holding him, until he had become calm and accepted that he wasn't going to get pushed. Then we went off and had a fun day.

2. Observe

Once you've got some distance and calmed down, if needed, the next step is to assess the situation. What is going on? Why has this occurred? Tantrums and emotional meltdowns are a form of nonverbal communication. Your child is trying to tell you something.

Too often parents ignore the message in the tantrum. They get so focused on trying to control the behaviour that they neglect to think about what's causing it. But without knowing what is being communicated, you can't deal with it as effectively in the moment or put preventative measures in place for the future.

Observation will tell you which kind of tantrum you are dealing with – emotional meltdown, situation tantrum or mock tantrum. Sometimes there might be a combination. For instance, your son starts to have a situational tantrum because he missed his nap due to the birthday party and then falls into a mock tantrum as he tries to manipulate you into letting him stay longer – the last thing he needs! You won't know what to do until you figure out what's going on for your child.

This is not necessarily easy. I worked once with a five-year-old boy in Oregon whose parents were going through a divorce. He was having emotional meltdowns because he was hurting and mock tantrums to try to get his own way as a result of his mother and father setting a bad example of disrespect to each other. His mother had to put her feelings of guilt over the breakup aside and deal with the mock tantrums when they occurred, as well as give lots of love and support when he had an emotional meltdown.

Like this mother had to, you need to work out what's going on. Is it an emotional meltdown triggered by grief because he lost his blankie or because he's still having trouble transitioning to nursery school? Or is it a situation tantrum because it's his lunch-time and you're stuck in a traffic jam? Or perhaps he wants to be able to do a puzzle and is frustrated because he can't quite figure it out. Maybe this is a mock tantrum because he's trying to manip-ulate you into giving him back the toy you just gave to his brother.

In this step, I quickly run down the options. I may think, 'Okay, this is a situation tantrum. The last time he ate was four hours ago. It's lunchtime, but I got behind on the errands. So now he's having a tantrum because his blood sugar levels are low. He needs to eat.' I think not only about the circumstances and the type of tantrum but also about the child. She may be quite

KNOW HOW:
TANTRUM SOS SHORTHAND

When I'm out and about and suddenly my little one is having a tantrum, what's the first thing I do?

- Identify the type of tantrum.

- Figure out why it's happening.

- Resolve it according to type.

sensitive and prone to emotional meltdowns. Or she's usually quite resilient but today is melting down over every little thing because something else is going on, like a move or other big change. Or she is very strong-willed and tantrums a lot and has thrown something, so she needs discipline.

3. Step In

You're calm and in control of yourself. You know what is going on for your child. Now it's time to step in and deal with the situation by implementing a plan of action (POA). Even if you choose to actively ignore the tantrum and walk into another room, you make up your mind to walk away. Rather than just react impulsively or ignore the whole thing and hope it ends soon, you consciously choose a path and follow it.

Remember, your child is trying to tell you something by tantruming. When you don't address it, it's like you've not listened to your child. If you don't address an emotional meltdown, then you aren't validating his feelings. If you don't address a situation tantrum, you aren't responding to his real needs, whether that's for food, sleep or a life skill that will give greater independence. When it's a mock tantrum, you're not setting a boundary.

Each type of tantrum requires a slightly different POA when you Step In, although in each situation, as I said before, the most important thing is to make sure your child is physically safe. The following SOS scenarios are based on my experience dealing with thousands of tantrums and they give you my plans of action for each type.

EMOTIONAL MELTDOWNS

In general, your two-and-a-half-year-old seems happy about having a new baby brother. But you notice that she is more demanding of your attention and if you are busy doing something for the baby and ask her to wait a few minutes, she has a complete crying fit, collapsing into a puddle on the floor. This happens several times a day and you are not sure how to handle it. You try to talk to her to find out why she's so upset, but that doesn't seem to work.

Step Back: Take a breath and don't react.

Observe: When is this happening? When she wants something from you and your attention is on the new baby? Do her tears seem to come from sadness rather than anger?

What do you want to achieve? Understanding what is going on for your child so you can respond appropriately.

Step In: Given the circumstances, this is most likely an emotional meltdown caused by sadness at having to share your attention and the adjustment to the new baby. When a child is melting down, often parents begin with rapid-fire questions: 'What's wrong? Why are you crying?' We want to be able to resolve the meltdown in sixty seconds, rather than have the patience to just be with him and wait till he's calm before we try to figure out what's going on. If he's very young, you know you'll have to guess, as he won't be able to tell you. You figure it out from the patterns of behaviour – she cries every time you give the baby attention, for instance. Rather than try to interrogate your little one, use my emotional meltdown POA:

Emotional Meltdown POA

1. Make sure he is in a place where he can't hurt himself, you or anyone else.
2. Because an emotional meltdown is caused by strong sad emotions, do not walk away or actively ignore your child. You want to sit with him so that he doesn't feel alone with his emotions and you can comfort his feelings: 'Of course you are upset your toy broke. It's sad.' 'Of course you're sad that Mummy left. She'll be back soon, though.'
3. When the crying subsides, use distraction to help him transition to a different mood. For instance, play with one of his toys so that he becomes interested. It's important to do this intentionally because often little children get stuck in their feelings. They're upset and don't know

how to get past where they are. You have to help them do that.

4. If he's caused destruction – thrown something or torn something up or hurt you (although if you've done step 1 properly, you've stayed out of the way) – then it's important to let him know that's not how we express our feelings and make him clean up the mess with you, say sorry and have a hug before moving on to the new activity.

5. Last but not least, reach out for cuddles, as emotionally he will need lots of affection and comforting. If he comes to you straightaway for cuddles, make sure you pacify him, but don't string out the drama. Moving on helps him to adapt to what has happened. In the same respect, if you go to cuddle him and he doesn't want to be cuddled, give him space while still being present.

After the storm has blown over, think again about what caused the emotional meltdown and what you might need to put in place. In this scenario, you want to make sure you create some time by yourself with your daughter – perhaps when the baby is asleep – so she recognises that she's not losing you, just sharing.

SITUATION TANTRUM

You're visiting a friend at their house and your three-year-old is late getting back home for her nap. First she fights getting out of the car, then she throws herself onto the snow-covered driveway and has a tantrum, complete with kicking and screaming. She

yelled so loud that the neighbors came out to see what was going
on. You were so embarrassed.

Step Back: Take a breath and don't react.
Observe: Can she hurt herself there? Is she in harm's way?
What do you want to achieve? Keeping her safe until the tantrum
blows over.

Step In: This is clearly a situation tantrum because she hasn't
had her nap. When you recognise the situation for what it is,
you can be more understanding. Rather than get angry or upset
with her, you can see how you could have prevented the situation by coming home earlier. Of course, it's not always your fault
– sometimes you're stuck in a situation that's not of your making. Regardless of the reason, once it's a full-blown tantrum, you
should deal with it using my situation tantrum POA:

Situation Tantrum POA

1. State that you know why she's upset: 'I know you're
   bored. We're almost done.' Distract if possible: 'Why
   don't you look at your book?'
2. If the tantrum is happening away from home and is disturbing others, remove her from the scene.
3. Cap the amount of time and energy you give to the situation. Otherwise it will lead your child to think the situation
   is negotiable and that can lead to mock tantrums.
4. If she hits, kicks you, spits or otherwise gets physical, use
   the Naughty Step technique.

5. Some children will come out of a tantrum faster if they are held. For others this only intensifies it. Experiment and see which works better.

6. Don't try to reason with her. She's not an adult and won't understand. In fact, do not speak at all except to validate her feelings at the beginning.

7. Once the tantrum is over, address the particular circumstance so that she will know what to expect in the future. If it was something she was trying to do, help her learn how to do it.

8. Next time you see her handle a situation better, make sure that you acknowledge her for it.

Once the tantrum wears itself out, address the immediate need that set it off in the first place. In this case, walk her into the house and into bed. Very clearly stipulate that tantrums are not the way to get things and praise her calm behaviour: 'I like this behaviour right now. This is what I like to see from you.' When you're descriptive in your praise, then she knows exactly what she's doing that's good and wants naturally to continue to do it. How you respond afterwards is really important in teaching your child to think about how she could achieve what she wanted without having a fit. You can do this very well from age three and a half onwards.

LIFE SKILL SITUATION TANTRUM

Your three-and-a-half-year-old wants to pour the juice into his glass, but he started to spill it, so you did it for him. This results

in him hitting you, then throwing himself onto the floor in a
tantrum.

Step Back: Take a breath and don't react.

Observe: Was this something you could have helped him do rather than do it for him? Have you helped him learn to pour? Has he been showing you in other ways that he wants more independence? How much do you do for him versus showing him what to do?

What do you want to achieve? His understanding that he can't hit, as well as his being able to pour on his own.

Step In: This is clearly a situation tantrum caused by anger at not being allowed to pour the juice. So first you would use the situation tantrum POA (page 267). Once the tantrum's over, put him on the Naughty Step for three minutes for hitting you. Then help him learn to pour: 'Okay, you got really angry about not being able to pour the juice. Let me help you. Put your hands here . . .' Make sure you're helping him learn his life skills rather than doing everything for him.

MOCK TANTRUMS

You are going down the crisps and sweets aisle at the supermarket and your almost-four-year-old heads straight for a bag of sweets. You tell him that he can't have that because it has too much sugar. He starts screaming at the top of his lungs, 'I want too much sugar, I want too much sugar.' You are mortified and try

to move on to another aisle. He trails behind, continuing to yell.
Now people are staring at you. You're extremely embarrassed and
unsure if you should give in or just ignore him.

Step Back: Take a breath and don't react.

Observe: Is it mock? In other words, is he trying to manipulate you? How many times have you given in to him when he's
done this before? Do you have clear rules and boundaries? Do
you follow through with consequences for naughty behaviour?

What do you want to achieve? Your child understanding that a
tantrum will not get him what he wants and no is no.

Step In: This is clearly a mock tantrum, which means you have
given in to a tantrum before and he's learned he can manipulate
you. That's understandable. It's human nature to want to stop anything that's overwhelming, loud, scary, embarrassing, shocking.

But if you want to end mock tantrums, you *absolutely, positively can't give in again.* This is a situation where you *must* be
absolutely disciplined in your response, no matter how much
your child acts out. Don't expect to do it right once and never see
a mock tantrum again. If they've been happening for a long time,
it will take time, energy and effort for your child to understand
that his acting out will not get him what he wants. Only by your
consistent, calm behaviour will you turn this situation around.

With mock tantrums, parents often pretend that it isn't happening and act as if they can't hear their child. I saw it happen just
the other day with a little girl in the toy store. She started screaming, 'I want it, I want it.' Her parents said nothing. So she just

screamed even louder. Now, would she have screamed louder if they had said no? Probably. But by pretending it wasn't happening, her parents didn't help her learn to accept no as the answer. You must always say no to a mock tantrum. Here's my mock tantrum POA:

Mock Tantrum POA

1. State your no and your reason why.
2. If it's happening in a public place and is disturbing others (church, a restaurant, etc.), remove her from the scene to a safe place if possible and stay with her.
3. Make it clear her behaviour is not going to get her what she wants: 'You need to stop this right now, because I'm not going to change my mind.'
4. If she acts out physically or verbally, give a warning: 'I know you're angry that you can't have what you want. But this is your warning. You can't talk to people like that [or you can't hit like that or yell like that]. If you carry on breaking the rules, you're going straight to the Naughty Step.' This is not unreasonable – remember, a mock tantrum is a manipulation she can control.
5. If she continues after the warning, use the Naughty Step technique (see page 218).
6. If there is no appropriate time or place to do the Naughty Step, explain that you will do it when you get home and be sure to follow through when you arrive. This is crucial because if there is no follow-through, she will soon not

believe your words. Remember, kids who mock-tantrum have the ability to stop, because these are mock tears.

Once again, after the storm is over, reflect on what you observed in step 2 of SOS. What is the underlying cause of your child's behaviour? Do you have clear rules in place and are you consistent in applying them?

TANTRUMS OUT AND ABOUT

Your two-and-a-half-year-old is at a birthday party. It's been going on for a while now and you can tell she's getting over-excited. The party is winding down, so you tell her you'll be going in a few minutes. When the time comes, she throws a hissy fit. You're mortified because she's doing this in front of a whole group of your friends.

Step Back: Take a breath and don't react.

Observe: Where is a quiet place you could remove her to deal with this?

What do you want to achieve? Getting your child calmed down and out the door as swiftly as possible.

Step In: I know that tantrums in public are particularly challenging for parents because other people are watching. While many parents want special techniques for dealing with tantrums in public, the truth is that consistency is the most important thing.

Dealing with tantrums in public is virtually the same as

handling them at home except you may have more safety issues and want to be as considerate to other people as possible. That means you need to find a quiet place to handle the meltdown or tantrum. At someone else's house it can be another room. At a shop it could be a bench or lawn outside. At a restaurant, church or event that is still going on, I recommend never using the car because the car makes a child feel like he's won and is going home.

The key to handling public tantrums, whether it's in a restaurant, at a family gathering or in a crowded supermarket, is the discipline to stay focused on resolving the tantrum using the appropriate steps I've outlined above, rather than worrying about what everybody else is thinking. Or if you can't help but think about what others are thinking, then use it to help you respond appropriately. The reality is that everybody's going to look and everybody's going to have an opinion, so you might as well be doing it right! Wouldn't you rather they were thinking, 'Oh, look! That lady's taking care of things over there' rather than 'Why won't that person do the responsible thing and deal with her child's tantrum?'

Appendix
Technique Troubleshooting Guide

SLEEPING

The Controlled Timed Crying Technique

1. What if she goes off to sleep fine but wakes up at 2:00 A.M.?
   Do the technique consistently until your child is sleeping entirely through the night. This should take you no longer than seven days max.

2. What should I do if my child won't lie down in the cot?
   You should proceed to continue with the technique as I've explained it. When you go in for a second time and she won't lie down, just make your 'shhh' noise and leave. It will seem harder for you to leave, but remember, if you pick her up it will make things worse. Stick to the technique.

3. What if my child doesn't cry straightaway – do I still double the time?

Wait until he cries and then start to double the time. Let him cry for a bit, as he may just be settling himself.

The Sleep Separation Technique

1. My child runs to the door when I am outside. What do I do?
   You will need to start back in the room and lengthen the amount of time before you begin to move away. So do three nights by her bed, then another three nights in the middle of the room and so forth.

2. I have twins. How do I position myself with two?
   In the middle of the two of them.

3. With this technique can I swap out with my partner?
   Only if it's a new night. The person who starts a particular night should remain to gain confidence in doing the technique.

The Stay in Bed Technique

1. My child is in her room playing with the lights on and not coming out of the room. What should I do?
   Remove the bulb if she keeps turning the light on after you have given a warning and proceed to follow through on discipline the next day for that behaviour. Trust me, it will change the next night!

2. What do I do when my triplets take turns coming downstairs?
   Deal with them separately.

3. How do I know when my child is having a real nightmare versus just wanting to get out of bed?
   Real nightmares are sporadic. They do not happen every night at the same time with excuses of everything under the sun for getting out of bed. Also, kids can be soothed to sleep if nightmares are real; they won't keep coming out of the bedroom every minute.

The Chimes Technique

1. My child has taken to calling us instead of coming into our room. What do we do?

   Do not go into her room. She'll come to you if need be. Most likely it's a ploy to get your attention, especially if you are doing this technique because of sleeping issues. When she does come in, proceed with the Stay in Bed technique.

2. My husband and I take turns. Is that okay?

   Yes! Better to take turns, ensuring that each of you gets a good night's sleep every other night!

3. My child comes into my bed on Saturday mornings. Should I be putting her back?

   If she does well staying in her bed during the week, then it is entirely up to you. Some families like to have weekend cuddles, especially those who work long hours all week. I don't think there's anything wrong with it as long as the rest of the week is good.

EATING

The Stay at Table Technique

1. My child wants her bunny to eat as well. Do I set a table for two?

   Yes – an imaginary one with pretend food. Remember, the bunny is eating well, so your child should too! Don't let the bunny take the blame for food not being eaten or bad behaviour.

SOCIALISATION

1. My child is six years old and doesn't want to walk anywhere. He keeps trying to get into his two-year-old sister's buggy. How do I encourage him to walk?

Take brief walks and build up his time out on foot – walk to shops, go to the park on foot. Let him know how proud you were of the trip you took together. Let him cycle or use a scooter too – they are both great for exercise.

2. When I get my two-year-old out of the buggy she keeps sitting down. Should I just put her back into the buggy?
    No. Encourage her to walk a little. Set a pace and mark where you will walk to, letting her know she can go back in when she gets there but will get back out again later too. Practise, lengthening the duration each time, until you are taking short trips without the buggy.

The Taking Turns Technique

1. My child cries all of the time until it is her turn. How do I stop it?
    You can't unless she chooses to be distracted by something else. Let it go. She will stop eventually when she trusts she will always get her turn too.

2. When my child gives up her turn, she loses interest and goes elsewhere. How do I reengage her?
    By show and tell. Explain the game and bring her back into it as if you were a great salesperson! Soon she will realise fun can be more than one.

The Time Sharing Technique

1. My child won't share the stuffed animal he sleeps with at night. Is that okay?
    Yes, it's okay to have something you don't share. I'm sure there are plenty of other toys he could share.

2. How do I get my older child to share the toys he's too big for with his younger sibling?

Explain that he is giving them up and have him give them to his sibling to share. When your firstborn says, 'It's mine,' you can say, 'It was before and now we're giving your younger sister a chance to enjoy it because you are a bigger boy.'

3. My child gives up the toy when her turn is over but then seconds later tries to snatch it back. How do I stop that behaviour?
   By teaching her how to have good behaviour while playing and that snatching is not kind. Give a warning if behaviour continues and then use a discipline technique if necessary.

The Involvement Technique

1. How do I stop my children from fighting over the shopping trolley?
   Explain that we take turns. Before you get into the supermarket, discuss whose turn it is.

2. How can I eliminate all the extra stuff the kids put into the trolley?
   Put a basket in the trolley. If they want something, they put it in the basket. At the end, they can each choose one thing. Or tell them outside the supermarket there will be no extra things today, only what is on the list.

EARLY LEARNING

The Play and Stay, Play Away Technique

1. My kid won't stay in a room at all without me.
   If this happens, play with him a bit first, then have him play something while you are in the room but not interacting with him. Practise this until you can leave him for a moment happily playing.

2. Why won't my child engage in play while I'm there playing with her?

    Maybe you take over too much. It would be great to sit back and allow your child to be the director. Prompt a story, for instance and then ask, 'Now what should I do?' as it will encourage her to use her imagination.

The Off the Hip Technique

1. My child cries and clings to my leg when I put him down . . . help!

    He will at first, but rest assured it will stop. Please continue with the technique and stay calm. If he sees you upset, it will confirm that he has something to worry about. Put toys in a wicker basket near where you spend most of your time so that he can play near you.

2. My son grabs my neck for cuddles while I am trying to talk. What should I do?

    Keep him at arm's length to talk, letting him know he can have cuddles after.

3. My child climbs up on me while I am on the floor trying to put her down.

    Gently stop her from doing so, while reassuring her you are not going anywhere, just getting on with things in the house while she plays and has fun. Stick with the technique!

NAUGHTY BEHAVIOUR

The Naughty Step Technique

1. My son keeps getting off the step. Should I just let it go after five times?

    No, no and no. He does that to test whether you will follow through. That's why it is vital you continue with each step of the technique. It's all about the follow-through.

2. Why won't my child say sorry?

   Because he is still angry or very stubborn and strong-willed. I believe the apology is an important part of respecting your rules. So please advise him he needs to stay on the step a few seconds more until you believe he has calmed down and then proceed to do the rest of the steps of the technique, right through to hugs and kisses.

3. My child says sorry straightaway once I put him on the step. Should I get him straight off?

   No, as he won't learn this way. The time lets him think about his actions and not think that just saying sorry with no true meaning will suffice. He needs to know you are in charge and will not put up with naughty behaviour.

The Sideline Technique

1. When I sideline my daughter during playdates, she keeps running back in to play.

   Put her back on the side and keep track of time. Remember it's not like the Naughty Step technique, which is for a specific amount of time. Just keep her out until you can feel her missing the activity. And don't forget to remind her of the behaviour you want to see.

2. My son tries to disturb play for others when on the sideline.

   Remind him why he is there and if need be, move to the Naughty Step technique if he won't listen.

3. My child will not come off the sideline. What should I do?

   That's his way of trying to gain control over the time-out. Let him know the time is up and he has your permission to get up and play. Ignore what he says. Some kids find it difficult; usually it is the strong-willed kids who sulk afterwards. Once he sees you're paying no attention, he'll get back into it again. After all, no kid wants to miss out.

The Confiscation Box Technique

1. My son tries to swap the toy that's in the box. Is that okay?
   No, make sure he doesn't. But it's a good indication that he understands what's happening. You must hold your ground to be respected.

2. After five minutes, my daughter tries to get the toy out and says she won't do it again. Should I give her the toy?
   No, you shouldn't. Remember she had already been given a warning to stop her naughty behaviour, so it's not as if she doesn't know what was expected.

3. I keep forgetting how long I keep the toy in the box for.
   The length of time is up to you, but you must be able to stick to it. For a two-year-old you can do an afternoon, for a three-year-old one day and one night and for four- and five-year-olds, two to three days. Make sure you write down when to bring it back out so as not to forget.

TANTRUMS

The Speaking Clock Technique

1. My kids try to negotiate the time. Should I do that?
   Can't blame them for trying! If you have trouble in this area, you must stick to what you say in order to be taken seriously.

2. My child pretends she can't hear me. How many times should I tell her?
   Normally parents will say it a few times to assure themselves their child heard what they asked. But if you are giving a warning, then it should be only once. Make sure your warnings and conversations are always face-to-face. It will help your toddler tremendously.

3. My son screams and clings to the swing when his time is up.

   Let's hope you are strong, because you will need to wrench those hands off the swing and go. Some kids get stronger when they're angry and upset. Just remain calm and move forward. Eventually he will realise that you come back and he gets to swing again.

Acknowledgments

I have always said that writing a parenting book gives me a chance to say the nitty gritties of everything that *you* the parent needs to know. Without having to worry about running out of TV time, it's truly a passionate part of the knowledge I give. My gratitude goes out to those who have assisted me so closely: Mary Jane Ryan, thank you so much for helping me transition what's from within to paper. You truly are an amazing star! Daniel Pangbourne, you did it again! Thank you for such a darling cover. Isabella, our little bubba, this is certainly one way to capture that cute face of yours forever! To Marnie, my editor, thank you for feeling so passionate about this book. Your dedication and focus is much appreciated. To Yfat, the captain of the ship, thank you for making sure the delivery of this book was in great hands. Cynthia, thank you for your support and enthusiasm which has often kept me afloat on long exhausting days! To the Ballantine team who believe, thank you. To my special close friends . . . support, love and loyalty. Thank you for always being there. To my loving family who nurture, uplift and bring much laughter (yes, you Matt and your hilarious impressions) to welcomed distraction: Dad, always there with your love and guidance, you are the best. Mum would be so proud! Last but not least I would like to mention a special thank you to millions of families around the world who continue to remind me with your love, support and heartfelt words how important this work is so that I may continue to help families in the best way I can.

Notes

CHAPTER 1: THE FIVE RULES OF DISCIPLINED PARENTING

11 **Recently I came across research that backs up my belief:** David Edie and Deborah Schmid, 'Brain Development and Early Learning', *Quality Matters: A Policy Brief Series on Early Care and Education,* Winter 2007, 2.

CHAPTER 2: WHY DISCIPLINE . . . AND WHY IT MATTERS

20 **Studies say – and I can confirm:** 'Child Discipline', American Humane Association, January 28, 2004, *www.americanhumane.org/children/stop-child-abuse/fact-sheets/child-discipline.html* (accessed August 20, 2012); 'Physical Discipline Makes Children Anxious and Aggressive', The Natural Child Project, n.d., *www.naturalchild.org/research/discipline.html* (accessed August 23, 2012).

20 **Researchers tell us that when parents fail to discipline:** 'Inconsistent Parenting Linked to Child Anti-social Behaviour', Family GP.com, February 27, 2012, *http://uk.lifestyle.yahoo.com/inconsistent-parenting-linked-child-anti-social-behaviour-120000658.html* (accessed August 20, 2012); Ron Bell, 'Discipline and Deviant Behaviour in Our Youth', Florida Dept. of Law Enforcement, August 1996, *www.fdle.state.fl.us/Content/getdoc/ce4ce538-9dc3-4b82-b963-6401f3b77a50/topics-juvenile-crime.aspx* (accessed August 20, 2012).

22 **In a recent survey, one-quarter of parents:** Laura Clark, 'The Death of

Discipline: Parents "Avoid Telling Children Off for Fear of Upsetting Them'", *Mail Online*, 17 February, 2010, *www.dailymail.co.uk/news/article-1251555/Parents-avoid-telling-children-fear-upsetting-new-survey-finds.html#ixzz2NvRsJL7j* (accessed 10 August, 2012).

22 **The parenting website BabyCenter recently did a survey:** 'BabyCenter Childhood Discipline Survey', October 2009, *www.babycenter.com* (accessed August 10, 2012).

26 **Thirty per cent of abused children:** 'National Child Abuse Statistics', ChildHelp, n.d., *www.childhelp.org/pages/statistics* (accessed September 13, 2012).

26 **Every day in this country five children:** Ibid.

CHAPTER 4: SLEEP RULES

50 **According to a National Sleep Foundation study:** '2008 Sleep in America Poll', National Sleep Foundation, 2008, *www.sleepfoundation.org* (accessed August 11, 2012).

51 **We're stretching our children's body clocks:** Po Bronson, 'Snooze or Lose', *New York Magazine*, October 7, 2007.

52 **Research has now confirmed what I have observed:** Louise M. O'Brien, 'The Neurocognitive Effects of Sleep Disruption in Children and Adolescents', *Child Adolescent Psychiatric Clinic North America 18 (2009): 813–823;* Gahan Fallone, Christine Acebo, J. Todd Arnedt, Ronald Seifer and Mary A. Carskadon, 'Effects of Acute Sleep Restriction on Behaviour, Sustained Attention and Response Inhibition in Children', *Perceptual and Motor Skills* 93 (2001): 213–229; Mary A. Brasch, Julie Reed and Beth Keen, 'Effects of Sleep Deficit in Children', Not My Kid, 2000–2008, *www.notmykid.org/media/12980/sleep%20disorders.pdf* (accessed August 11, 2012).

53 **Dr Monique LeBourgeois of Brown University:** Bronson, 'Snooze or Lose'.

54 **That's why there are studies showing an increase:** Denise Mann, 'Can Better Sleep Mean Catching Fewer Colds?' WebMD, January 19, 2010, *www.webmd.com/sleep-disorders/excessive-sleepiness-10/immune-system-lack-of-sleep?* (accessed August 11, 2012).

54 **New research at the UCLA School of Public Health:** Christina Boufis, 'Can Your Child's Sleep Habits Make Him Gain Weight?' WebMD, March 23, 2011, *www.webmd.com/parenting/features/can-your-childs-sleep-habits-make-him-gain-weight* (accessed August 11, 2012).

54 **It is estimated that parents lose about two hundred hours:** O'Brien, *'The Neurocognitive Effects of Sleep Disruption', 813.*

56 **In a study done on adults, a scientist:** Bronson, 'Snooze or Lose', 8.

CHAPTER 6: FOOD RULES

86 **In a sample of obese children five to seventeen years old:** 'Childhood Obesity Facts', Center for Disease Control and Prevention, February 19, 2013, *www.cdc.gov/healthyyouth/obesity/facts.htm* (accessed March 18, 2013).

91 **This may be harder than it seems:** Pamela Peeke, *Fit to Live (*New York: Rodale, 2007), 88.

91 **Just a few examples of how much bigger servings:** 'Portion Distortion', National Heart, Lung and Blood Institute Obesity Education Initiative PowerPoint slides, 2003, 2004, *http://hp2010.nhlbihin.net/portion* (accessed August 15, 2013); Peeke, *Fit to Live*, 88.

91 **The average adult is eating 530 more calories:** Peeke, *Fit to Live*, 88.

CHAPTER 10: EARLY LEARNING RULES

159 **85 per cent of his brain develops:** David Edie and Deborah Schmid, 'Brain Development and Early Learning', *Quality Matters: A Policy Brief Series on Early Care and Education,* Winter 2007, 1.

160 **Here's just one example of how important:** 'Brain Research', League of Education Voters, n.d., *www.educationvoters.org/brain research,* 2 (accessed August 23, 2012).

160 **Children with early education show better attachment:** Ibid.

162 **Research shows that the more parents talk:** 'Brain Development', First 5 California, n.d., *www.ccfc.ca.gov/parents/learning-center/brain-development/ ?a=Brain%20Development&t=1345744963346#/?a=Brain%20Development* (August 24, 2012); 'Brain Development and Early Learning'; 'Child Development and Early Learning', Facts for Life, n.d., *www.factsforlifeglobal .org/03* (accessed *August 24, 2012).*

162 **In addition, physical movement is crucial for brain development:** Len Kravitz, 'Exercise and the Brain: It Will Make You Want to Work Out', *IDEA Fitness Journal* 7, no. 2 (February 2010); Gretchen Reynolds, 'Phys Ed: Can Exercise Make Kids Smarter?' *New York Times,* September 15, 2010.

163 **Children with poor fine motor skills have been shown:** 'Advantages of Addressing Fine Motor Skills in Early Childhood', Emerge: A Child's Place, May 2009 newsletter, *http://emergeachildsplace.com/documents/ newsletters/2009-May-Fine-Motor-Skills-Preschoolers.pdf* (accessed August 24, 2012).

165 **The current recommendation:** 'The Benefits of Limiting TV', Healthy-Children.org, American Academy of Pediatrics, January 31, 2013, *www .healthychildren.org/English/family-life/Media/Pages/The-Benefits-of-Limiting -TV.aspx* (March 18, 2013).

165 **Plus research has linked TV watching:** 'How TV Affects Your Child',

Kids Health, October 2011, *http://kidshealth.org/parent/positive/family/tv_affects_child.html* (accessed August 24, 2012).

183 **Researchers have discovered that in order to develop:** Edie and Schmid, 'Brain Development and Early Learning', 1.

CHAPTER 11: EARLY LEARNING SOS

191 **Recently my findings were backed up by new:** Laura Neergaard, 'Babies Learn to Talk by Reading Lips, New Research Suggests', Huffington Post, January 16, 2012, *www.huffingtonpost.com/2012/01/16/babies-learning-to-talk_n_1209219.html* (accessed August 25, 2012)

CHAPTER 12: GOOD BEHAVIOUR RULES

208 **Recently brain scientists have unlocked:** 'Giving Praise', MindTools, n.d., *www.mindtools.com/pages/article/giving-praise.htm* (accessed August 25, 2012).

CHAPTER 15: TANTRUM SOS

258 **Whichever of these responses is triggered:** Navneet Ahuja, Wutyi Thwe Myat, Alexandra Cervantes and Natasha Zahn, 'Amygdala Hijack', Neuroscience Fundamentals, n.d., *http://neurosciencefundamentals.unsw.wikispaces.net/The+limbic+System* (accessed August 27, 2012).

Index

ABOUT THE AUTHOR

With more than twenty-five years as a parental expert and former nanny, JO FROST is a global household name. Her TV shows *Supernanny, Extreme Parental Guidance* and *Family S.O.S. with Jo Frost* have received huge international acclaim. She has written seven parenting books, including the *Sunday Times* bestselling *Confident Toddler Care,* which have been translated into many languages, inspiring families throughout the world.

www.jofrost.com

@Jo_Frost